FAMILY

A Safe Haven in a World of Turbulence

FAMILY

A Safe Haven in a World of Turbulence

Edited by

Mustafa Mencüketin

BLUE DOME

Copyright © 2013 by Blue Dome Press

15 14 13 12   1 2 3 4

Fountain Books

Published by Blue Dome Press

345 Clifton Ave., Clifton,

NJ, 07011, USA

www.bluedomepress.com

Library of Congress Cataloging-in-Publication Data Available

ISBN: 978-1-935295-24-2

Printed by

Çağlayan A.Ş., Izmir - Turkey

CONTENTS

Editor's Preface

The majority of human population, as universally agreed, know that Adam, the first man, and Eve, the first woman, were created together at the very beginning of human existence, and that this noble creation is the first indication that marriage and building a family are an essential and natural part of life. Naturally, reproduction is the most sacred outcome of this union. From a sociological perspective, the soundest foundation for a nation is a family in which material and spiritual happiness flows, for such a family serves as a sacred school that raises virtuous individuals. The future of every individual is closely related to the impressions and influences experienced during childhood and youth. The word "home" is used according to the people residing in it. Individuals are considered happy to the degree that they share core human values. A home becomes a home because of its inhabitants who deserve to be fortunate as members of a family.

The lifestyle led today is one of modernity, a modern way of living that reached its peak during the development stage of Western civilization. With the rise of modernity—systematically emerged as an intellectual result of 17th Century Enlightenment and a political consequence of the French Revolution and an economical end of the Industrial Revolution— almost all people have been undergoing a malicious process of imposition by means of states, press, media or educational systems. The semantic shifts and radical changes in life philosophies caused by modernism have rapidly worn out the values pertaining "the family." The strategists of global world order have begun to annihilate societies through psychological wars via "the family"; and the fact that popular culture has exposed confidentiality has provided the necessary means for the gradual fade-away of "the family".

Offering a particular world view, understanding of economics, popular trademarks, and ways of consumption, modernity compels "modern" and "isolated" types of relationships that ostracize "the family" from its territories as it is the strongest station of resistance to so-called virtues of modernity. In short, modernism simply tears to shreds "the family" as masses of people that have emigrated to metropolises and undergone economic woes are now fully imprisoned by the concepts of "the nuclear family", that is a mere euphemism for "lost family", and a tendency of a life led independent from "the family".

This collection of articles that have been published afore on Fountain Magazine seeks reasonable answers to the vital question of how a new ideal family could be constructed without passing over the spirit of time, be it "modern or post-modern times". The articles address the essential issues regarding "the family" and the vitality of upbringing the fruits of it—particularly, the generation of Internet and the age of technology. To enhance the readers understanding within the context of family, the writers offer various perspectives and approaches to "the family". M. A. Şahin discusses "Training in the Home", Hasan Aydınlı offers "Appropriate Messages in Child Training", Sermed Öğretim philosophies on "Resonant Egos and the Art of Married Life", Mehmet Köylü asks "Why Is Internet Control Necessary?" to guide parents to a controlled internet access, while Harun Avcı offers some effective ways to enable children to love reading. Overall, all the articles echo the same message: Long live our family, long live happy kids and parents!

The Problems of Today's Young

Fethullah Gülen

When the problems of the young are discussed, some turn away with indifference, supposing that many useless things, discussed many times before, will be repeated. In their view, what needs be done with the young is simply to seal up their mouths, to shut them up, to fetter their heads and minds, and compel them to obey social rules. Whenever they show signs of rebellion, they should severely be punished, either by imprisonment, exile or beating or, when necessary, by hanging on the gallows. There are some others, on the other hand, who are tired of dealing with this vital issue in the face of the continuing indiscretions of the young and their bad behavior.

Danilevsky's view that the transference of civilizations from one country to another is impossible has received a general welcome from sociologists. Bediüzzaman Said Nursi expressed another excellent view that since Islam is the last religion that encompasses all the truths contained by the previous Divinely revealed religions, one who gives up Islam is like spoilt butter, while one who gives up either of the other religions is like spoilt milk, for those religions were already corrupted. As is known, spoilt butter cannot be eaten, whereas spoilt milk can be. The youth of Muslim countries are victims of both the useless efforts to import Western civilization into their countries and the rejection of Islam on a large scale, while the youth of the West suffer from the corruption and denunciation of Christianity and from suffocating materialism. Some of our intellectuals have preferred to weep in the face of the pitiful condition of the young. Pained to witness the collapse of a once glorious state, some sighed:

I have become like the owl which laments over ruins,

When I have seen this once paradise-like land in its autumn.

If I lived in the time of roses I'd become the nightingale to celebrate it;

O Lord! I wish you had sent me to the world earlier!

11

However, lamenting without doing anything practical will be of no use. In order to solve the problems of the young, what must be done first is to diagnose those problems well. What is the origin of those problems? Are the young responsible for them? Why are those problems so grave today, graver than in any other period of history? Did the young come to the world as they are, or were they not, rather, brought up and educated in our homes and schools? Are the problems which we see as originating from the young really their problems or are we ourselves responsible for them?

Man comes to the world like a raw metal to be wrought, without knowing anything about life. When an animal comes to the world, it comes equipped with all it will need during its life. Some of them learn and are adapted to the conditions of life in a few minutes or hours. A sparrow or a bee acquires in so short a time as twenty days all the faculties it needs to be fully active and mature; a human by contrast needs about twenty years. This means that the main tasks in life of an animal and a human are quite different. Man's basic duty in life is to find the true way in thinking and believing and, by using his outer and inner faculties like the five external senses and the intellect, the heart and feelings, to attain physical, intellectual, spiritual and moral perfection. Unless this can be done, it is inevitable that we must face many problems in life. We should not forget that all problems originate from man and end with him.

In order to diagnose the problems of the young, we must discover the character of man and know it very well. As long as man remains unknown, the problems concerning him will remain unsolved. To know man requires being able to answer the vital questions every individual asks himself: Who am I? Where do I come from? Who has sent me to this world and why? What is the purpose for my life? What does death ask of me? What is my final destination in life? Unless man can find convincing answers to such questions, answers that will make him at peace, man can neither find true happiness nor will it be possible to solve his problems.

The first school where man receives the necessary education in order to be perfected and find the answers to the questions above is the home. Both for the raising of a healthy generation and the continuation of a healthy social system or structure, the home is of vital importance. However important a good school is for the education of man, the responsibility of home cannot be restricted to the period before school, rather, it continues throughout ones whole life. A man receives the first impressions in his family. Those impressions cannot be easily deleted in later phases of life; rather, they are of a kind to show their effect throughout life. Further, the control of the family over the child exerted in the garden, among other children and toys, is to be continued at school among friends, among books and in other places visited. The function of parents in bringing up their children is like the duty of a shepherd to his flock: as a shepherd may be regarded as having done his duty so long as he finds good pastures for his flock, prevents them from grazing in fields belonging to others and protects them against dangers, so too must the parents keep their children within lawful courses, shape them in good manners and virtues, prepare them for the future phases of their lives, educate them to be useful members of the society, and enable them to seek eternal happiness in the eternal world.

For a man to receive a good education at home, a healthy family life should be established and preserved. For this reason, marriage should not be seen as something to enter into for mere pleasure. One should marry to form a healthy family life and thereby contribute to the permanence of one's nation in particular and the human population in general, and to restrain one's carnal desires. Since the first condition of peace, happiness and security at home is mutual accord between the spouses, the accord in thinking, morals and belief, the couples who have decided to marry should know each other very well and consider the purity of feelings, chastity, morality, and being virtuous rather than wealth and physical charm. The condition of children, who grow up in a house where parents repel each other like the particles charged with the same sort of electricity, is truly heart-rending. Discord between parents causes children to grow up not being able to get on well with others.

There are many families founded on sound logic and reasoning in reliance upon God. They function like a good school during one's life and secure the future of their nation by means of the "students" they educate. For this reason, the nations which have succeeded in making homes into schools and schools into homes have guaranteed the peace and happiness of future generations. A building deserves to be called a "home" only if its inhabitants have the necessary human values. In the family, the elders should behave toward those younger than them with compassion and the younger ones should show respect for their elders. Particularly, parents should love and respect each other and treat their children with compassion and due consideration of their feelings. Without compassion, a mercy that envelops the universe warmly and resonates in man as a melody of creation, it is impossible to raise children towards true humanity. Parents should also treat their children justly and should not discriminate between them. They should not bring up their children jealous of one another. They should never shake their children's trust and confidence in them.

Parents should not neglect to give their children good, meaningful names, say greetings to them when they come in and go out of the home, assign to their children certain things like particular rooms, beds and so on, follow their games and work genuinely, frequently ask about their health and problems, share their joys and sorrows, and occasionally embrace and kiss them. Although they should make their children feel that they are aware of the wrong they do and sometimes punish them lightly, children should also feel that the breeze of forgiveness and tolerance blows in their home.

School

After the home, the school is so vital a part of the making of human beings that it may be considered as a laboratory in which an elixir is offered which can prevent or heal the ills of life, and teachers are the masters by whose skills and wisdom the elixir is prepared and administered. The school is a place of learning where everything related to this life and the next can be learnt. It can shed light on vital ideas and events and enable its students to understand their natural and human environment. It can also quickly open the way to unveiling the meaning of things and events, which leads man to wholeness of thought and contemplation. In essence the school is a kind of place of worship whose "holy men" are teachers.

Good schools worthy of the name are pavilions of angels, which develop feelings of virtue in their pupils and lead them to achieve nobility of mind and spirit. As to the others, however soundly built they may appear, they are in fact ruins, for they instil false ideas into their pupils, turning them into monsters. Such schools are nests of snakes, and we should be consumed with shame that they are called places of learning. As it is in the school that life, flowing outside in so many different directions, acquires a stable character and identity, so too it is in the school that a child is cast in his or her true mould and attains to the mysteries of personality. Just as a wide, full river gains force as it flows in a narrow channel, so too, the flowing of life in undirected ways is channelled into unity by means of the school. In like manner, a fruit is a manifestation of unity growing out of the fruit-tree's diversity.

School is thought to be relevant only in a particular phase of life. However, it is much more than that. It is essentially the "theatre" in which all the scattered things of the universe are displayed together. It provides its pupils with the possibilities of continuous reading and speaks even when it is silent. Because of that, although it seems to occupy one phase of life, the school actually dominates all times and events. Every pupil re-enacts during the rest of their life what he or she has learnt at school and derives continuous influence therefrom. What is learned or acquired at school may either be creativity and goal-setting or specific skills and realities. But what is of importance here is that everything acquired must, in some mysterious way, be the key to closed doors, and guidance to the ways of virtue.

Information rightly acquired at school and fully internalized by the self, is a means by which the individual rises beyond the clouds of this gross world of matter and reaches the borders of eternity. Information not fully internalized by the self is no more than a burden loaded upon the pupil's back. It is a burden of responsibility on its owner, and a devil which confuses the mind. That kind of information which has been memorized but not fully digested does not provide light to the mind and elevation to the spirit, but remains simply a nuisance to the self.

The best sort of knowledge to be acquired in the school must be such that it enables pupils to connect happenings in the outer world to their inner experience. The teacher must be a guide who can give insight into what is experienced. No doubt the best guide—and one that continually repeats its lessons—is life itself. Nevertheless, those who do not know how to take a lesson directly from life need some intermediaries. These intermediaries are the teachers, for it is they who provide the link between life and the self, and interpret the manifestations of life's happenings.

The mass media can communicate information to human beings, but they can never teach real life. Teachers are irreplaceable in this respect. It is the teachers alone who find a way to the heart of the pupil and leave indelible imprints upon his or her mind. Teachers who reflect deeply upon, and impart the truths will be able to provide good examples for their pupils and teach them the aims of the sciences. They will test the information they are going to pass on to their pupils through the refinement of their own minds, not by such Western methods as thought today to provide superficial answers to everything. The students of Prophet Jesus, upon him be peace, learnt from him how to risk their lives for the sake of their cause and were able to endure being thrown into the mouths of lions—they knew that their master had persisted with his teachings even in the face of death threats. Those who put their hopes on, and gave their hearts to, the Prophet Muhammad, the greatest exemplar of humanity, upon him be peace and blessings, realized that suffering for the sake of truth resulted in peace and salvation. His students observed their master, wishing peace and felicity for his enemies even when he had been severely injured by them.

A good lesson is what the real teacher teaches at school. This lesson not only provides the pupil with something, but it also elevates him or

her into the presence of the unknown. The pupil thus acquires a penetrating vision into the reality of things and sees each event as a sign of the unseen worlds. At such a school, one is neither tired of learning nor teaching, because the pupils, through the increasing zeal of their teacher, sometimes rise to the level of stars. Sometimes their consciousness overflows the boundaries of ordinary life, brimming with wonder at what they have thought or felt or experienced.

The real teacher seizes the landmarks of events and happenings and tries to identify the truth in everything, expounding it by using every possibility. Rousseau's teacher was his conscience; Kant's was his conscience together with reason... In the school of Rumi and Yunus, the teacher was Prophet Muhammad, upon him be peace and blessings. The Qur'an is the recitation, its words are Divine lessons—they are not ordinary words but mysterious ones surpassing all others, and they manifest the highest unity in multiplicity. A good school is a holy place where the light of the Qur'an will be focused, and the teacher is the magic master of this mysterious laboratory. The only true master is one who will save us from centuries-old pains, and, by the strength of his wisdom, remove the darkness covering our horizon.

Training in the Home

■ M. A. Şahin

Bringing up children successfully means caring for them so that they grow up to be independent, responsible human beings. This entails training them—as much through example as through precept—in a rounded and balanced way which pays due attention to all aspects of their physical as well as moral well-being. It means providing a general education which combines preparation for life in this world and life in the hereafter, which minimizes disorder and confusion in the children's minds and carries them towards harmony and unity of the whole range of human faculties, from the physical and emotional to the psychological and spiritual.

Emphasis on bodily perfection while neglecting moral and spiritual development is not a part of Islamic tradition. Equally, emphasis on spiritual training based upon contempt or denial of bodily life is not a part of Islamic tradition. Islam is, in almost every respect, characterized by the quest for balance, harmony and unity of means and ends. Therefore, Islam is not a way of either denial or indulgence, but a way of discipline.

Discipline and orderliness with sufficient flexibility to allow for spontaneity of actions and feelings are the defining general characteristic of an Islamic upbringing. Children who do not grow up in an atmosphere of orderliness and self-control are unlikely, as adults, to meet their responsibilities in a consistently calm and dignified manner. Rather, they are likely to lead strained and miserable lives, however successful they may become later in their working lives. By way of illustrating Islamic upbringing, we shall focus discussion here on the familiar areas of eating and sleeping habits and the importance of cleanliness.

In general, if a family's daily routine is steady and consistent, the children's lives and characters will follow a similarly ordered pattern, both within the home and outside. If not, they will most probably be disorganized, lacking in will and concentration, and tend to fits of antisocial behavior. Children imbibe orderliness and discipline from the adults

immediately around them and develop strong character. If, on the other hand, they grow up in a confused, unstable, haphazard atmosphere, they too will become confused and unstable, liable to aimlessness and depressions, and all the unhappy consequences of these.

In practice, orderliness means that children know when they are expected home, and how their time is normally spent when they are at home and outside the home. They should learn as early as possible how to allocate their time between work and play so that what they have to do is done in time and they enjoy their lives. They should learn how to make moral choices, how to co-operate within the family and with others outside the family. They should learn the importance of regular prayer and aided to mature a taste for contemplation and devotion to God. They should be brought up to be, as developed human beings are, both active and reflective. They should understand the importance of their own lives while learning, through good manners and awareness of the needs and feelings of others, the value of humility.

Eating Habits

The eating habits of a family should be based on sound dietary principles. This means having regular eating times, avoiding excess, choosing as far as practicable to eat in company (rather than alone) and sharing with others (rather than preferring oneself); avoiding those things that are harmful to the mind, the will and the body (for example, rushing food in a disrespectful manner); and it means cleanliness, both of the food consumed and the way it is consumed.

In this respect, to start eating again without fully digesting what has already been eaten, that is, eating randomly and always keeping the mouth busy and the stomach full is injurious to the body and poisonous, even lethal, to the will. The Creator has expressed strong dislike of such manners. Any food eaten in the wrong way is harmful, but worst of all is to eat harmful food in a harmful way.

Prodigality, or wasteful excess, is an act of disrespect and ingratitude for the Creator's infinite blessings. Those who over-indulge themselves puzzle and confound their appetite, or they drown in food without ever tasting contentment or satisfaction. Wastefulness is such an offence and so ruinous to the heart and soul that the individual will, eventually, be prepared to eat anything and everything, regardless of whether it is permitted or prohibited, whether he needs it or not, even of whether he likes it or not.

Sensible diet is a matter of discipline and awareness of the nutritional and social values of good manners. A family who can teach their children self-control in what and how they eat must be considered most fortunate, for they have laid the foundations for their children's spiritual progress as well as of the health of their bodies. Children should therefore be taught the aims and principles of sensible diet so that they begin to choose good habits for themselves and not simply copy the habits to which they are exposed. If parents are unable to articulate or explain the importance of diet and nutrition, they should ask a competent and knowledgeable person to do so for them.

Sleeping Hours

To discipline sleeping habits is of as much importance as disciplining eating habits. We need to rest at particular times in order to stay healthy

and have command of all our resources— physical, mental, emotional and psychological. The balance and stability of our personalities depends upon non-disruptive patterns of working and resting. The greater part of the day should be set aside for working and the night for rest and sleep. It is not reasonable to change this order. Trying to change it means risking tensions and conflict in social relationships, contradicting the natural rhythm of the universe and ruining one's health. It will be useful to mention a few principles for resting and sleeping hours which might be suitable for everyone:

a) the routines of family members should be coordinated with each other. If resting and sleeping hours are orderly, most of the work needed to maintain a happy family has been done. Disorderly sleeping habits affect eating times, affect mood and temperament, and give rise to many insoluble difficulties and disputes.

b) the lives of neighbors should correspond with each other. Otherwise they disrupt each other's working and resting periods.

c) particular times should be allocated to resting and working. Randomly changing resting and working hours will disrupt sleeping patterns, which, in turn, negatively affects both one's rest and work.

d) whatever injures sleep should be avoided. Sometimes a few cups of tea, sometimes a little food, sometimes boredom, may ruin a night and therefore the working day that follows it.

Cleanliness

It is commonly accepted that habits of cleanliness are passed from parents to children. Imitation is a vital part of human development—it must be so as human beings have so much that they need to learn quickly in order to take their place in adult life. Children will believe in the importance of cleanliness if they see it in their immediate environment, if they see the adults around them keeping themselves clean, and if cleanliness is stressed as something necessary and desirable. Conversely, if they see no effort to maintain tidiness and cleanliness, they will grow up negligent of their responsibility to be personally clean and to keep their immediate surroundings in order.

The importance of cleanliness could not have been more emphasized in a culture than it has been in Islam. Worship in Islam is a commitment of the body as well as the mind and spirit. A part of the dignity of being a Muslim worshipper is to do partial ablution (washing the normally exposed parts of the body) before each of the five obligatory prayers and a full ablution (or bath) at least once a week. In addition, it is strongly commended, almost obligatory, to wash one's hands before and after meals, not to touch the mouth as soon as one wakes up from sleep but only after washing them, to keep one's hair and nails properly trimmed and clean, etc.

In sum, orderliness and discipline are not social devices to burden the individual and enforce a rigidly patterned conformity. Rather, they are the means to ensure the health of body and mind and will, the stability of the whole character, so that the individual acquires the grace and dignity of person which can only come from strength based upon self-control. The role of the family in equipping children for such dignity with and in their lives is decisive.

Appropriate Messages in Child Training

■ Hasan Aydınlı

An old Chinese proverb says that: "Give a man a fish and you feed him for a day. Teach him to fish and you feed him for the rest of his life." This proverb points out the importance of education. There is perhaps no other subject that has greater importance than the education of children. This is the only way to shape the future. It is almost impossible to meet someone who would disagree with this point of view, yet there are many different approaches to education. Governments spend huge sums of money to build reliable and long-lasting training programs. Pedagogues are relentlessly working on this subject to find the best and most appropriate ways to educate children.

The human learning process begins with birth. The person who starts to understand their body, organs, environment, and the world in this first stage enhances their skills by practicing them within the limits of the capabilities that God has given. With the help of the senses such as hearing, seeing, touching, and smelling, the amount of knowledge proliferates rapidly. Every warning and message that reaches us is an important factor in helping learning, developing consciousness, and becoming aware of life. While the development of the intelligence and mental activity of children who lack sufficient warnings and messages becomes slower, the development of the ones who are overloaded is dispersed. It must be kept in mind that the fastest growing system in a child's body during the first three years of life is the nervous system. Therefore, appropriate messages must be provided very early on, even from the very beginning of the pregnancy.

Messages that are received through the sense of hearing have a significant importance in child education. The mental development of children who have received ample and appropriate messages is more significant and positive. It is a well-known fact that even in the earliest stages of pregnancy the baby can distinguish the mother's voice, and is relaxed via the sense of hearing; this sense starts to develop at the very beginning of pregnancy. Unfortunately, some parents turn the television or the radio on in the baby's room, frequently letting them listen to it. However,

what is best for the baby is to have suitable audio incentives that can be easily understood. On the other hand, to remain silent when with a baby for a long time will negatively affect the language learning process. A conversation between parents in a relaxed and gentle tone, talking about pleasant things, for example, a beautiful poem, the sound of someone reading the Qur'an, or the sound of the *adhan* coming from the minarets, are all useful messages for babies.

Messages received through the sense of sight are as important as those received through hearing. Humans recognize nature and themselves by seeing, touching, and trying. Although the visual capabilities of a baby develop in the womb, it takes some six months for sight to reach an appropriate level. Babies accept everything that they see during this time as training material. Everything that is seen has an important role in forming the baby's personality. Parents must always be good models for their children, acting in commendable ways. It is a well-known fact that babies pay attention to their parents' behavior. Since imitation is one of the earliest learning techniques; parents should remember to behave in a way that they want their children to behave. Helping each other, forgiveness, responsibility, hard-work, empathy, and correct behavior are quali-

ties that parents should demonstrate. Seeing a parent working hard, reading, and praying will help the conscience of the child to develop. Fighting, noise, and angry words will negatively affect the development.

Messages sent through meta-communication are more effective. For example, in an advertisement of a certain product, the fact that people using that product are smiling is more important than the properties of the product. This is because such behavior attaches the message "you will be happier when you use it." For children, living in a positive environment helps them to observe correct models. Since they use the very first form of learning—that is, imitation—providing good examples of behavior is extremely important. In the learning process, sight is one of the most frequently used methods. Therefore, parents must display appropriate behavior to help their children to learn. Displaying correct behavior is more effective than explaining what correct behavior is.

The environment in which we live has a great importance in the education of children. The school that is chosen for children must be considered from different aspects. Most people never forget their first teacher; this is one of the milestones in our lives. The teacher starts to shape our personalities at an early age. Therefore, choosing the right teacher, someone who is not only capable, but is also virtuous and pleasant, is of great importance. The teacher's style of dressing, way of talking, their reaction to stimulus and their behavior tells us more than the teacher can; these are also the most effective means of sending messages to our children.

The children's group of friends is another environment that needs to be monitored carefully. Having the right friends positively affects the development of the personality of the child, while having inappropriate friends will have negative effects. Many parents cannot attain positive results, despite all their efforts in education, merely because they have forgotten the importance of the peer group on the child. Starting from the ages 6–7, the effect of friends increases gradually, peaking in the teenage years.

The effect of the media on children is indisputable, especially in today's world. We can see violence, fear, and a lack of moral values in our children; these are all the effects of media. It is known that in cases where babies spend much time watching television, these children fail to develop their linguistic skills and become withdrawn from society. The massive visual or audio input from television can cause significant problems in the psychological development of the child. Some parents allow their children to watch advertisements, as they are unaware of this fact. In child education, especially in the early stages, parents must be very careful to combat the inappropriate stimuli of the television and computer. During that period the baby needs the parents' interest, love, conversation, and physical closeness more than they need the picture on the television or computer. Parents must remember that every stimulus during these stages has a long-lasting effect throughout the child's life. Therefore, the stimuli given to the child must be appropriate.

As a drop of water can shape a rock by falling on it every day, so can appropriate or inappropriate messages shape the personality of a child over time. All the messages must be suitable to the age; they must contribute to the child's development. They must be neither too difficult, nor incomplete and insufficient. They must be in close relation with the environment. They must not contain opposing messages, and they must not impose fear or despair.

As a result, in the education of the child, parents, educators and teachers must provide appropriate, sufficient, and positive warnings and messages for children.

Parenting Styles: How They Affect Children

■ Süheyla Saraç

P arenting is a most challenging yet rewarding experience. Baumrind, who studied parenting styles during the early 1960s, concluded that they differ in four important areas: parents' warmth/nurturance, discipline strategy, communication skills, and expectations of maturity. She posited three types of parenting styles: authoritarian, permissive, and authoritative (Berger 2001). Parents are the major influence in their children's lives. Thus their perception of how children think, and should be raised is crucial in determining children's behavior. Other factors, such as genes, peers, culture, gender, and financial status, are of lesser importance. Studies reveal a correlation between parenting styles and school competence, delinquency, violence, sexual activity, antisocial behavior, alcohol and substance abuse, depression, anxiety, and self-perception.

Authoritarian Parents

Authoritarian parenting, also termed dictatorial or harsh, is low on warmth/nurturance, strict on discipline, high in parent-to-child communication but low in child-to-parent communication, and high on expectation. This style has been predominant throughout Western history: "It was effective in status quo times, for example in agrarian-industrial societies" (Dinwiddie 1995). Authoritarian parents show little affection and "seem aloof from their children" (Berger 2001, 283). Parents instruct and order, do not consider the children's opinion as a group, and discourage verbal give-and-take (Gonzalez-Mena 1993). Obedience, respect, and tradition are highly valued. Rules are non-negotiable, parents are always right, and disobedient children are punished-often physically. However, parents "do not cross the line to physical abuse" (Berger 2001, 283). As children obey their parents in order to avoid punishment, they become passive. Authoritarian parents also expect a level of maturity higher than the norm for their child's particular age group: "The authoritarian parents assign the child the same responsibilities as adults" (Scarr, Wein-

berg, and Levine 1986, 306). Responsiveness is low, as the approach is parent-centered and stresses the parent's needs.

This almost non-interactive style has serious developmental drawbacks (Daniel, Wassell, and Gilligan 1999). Children are more susceptible to antisocial peer pressure during adolescence, a time when peer influence is the greatest (Collins et al. 2000); learn not to discuss issues with their parents (why bother if you are always wrong or ignored?); and are influenced greatly by their peers. Often frustrated, they distance themselves from their parents by rebelling against the latter's values and beliefs.

Steinberg et al. (1994) reveals that boys in this category have the highest level of violence. Steinberg (1996) shows that these teenagers are less self-reliant, persistent, and socially poised, and have lower self-esteem. In addition, there is a strong inverse correlation between such authoritarianism and good grades. Other research indicates that they lack social competence and rarely initiate activities: "They show less intellectual curiosity, are not spontaneous and usually rely on the voice of authority" (Parenting n.d.).

Permissive Parents

Permissive parenting, also labeled as neglectful or disengaged parenting, is high on warmth, very low on discipline and structure, low in parent-to-child communication but high in child-to-parent communication, and low on expectation. This style was popular in the 1950s and 1960s. The fact that many German children and adults had followed Hitler led people to attribute this to Germany's authoritarian home environment, which demanded unquestioning obedience. Thus their parents "conditioned" them for Hitler. (Dinwiddie 1995). Hoping to counteract such undesirable side-effects, they became permissive.

Permissive parents are nurturing, warm, and accepting. Their main concerns are to let children express their creativity and individuality and to make them happy (Neal 2000), in the belief that this will teach them right from wrong (Berger 2001). Permissive parents find it hard to set clear limits, provide structure, are inconsistent disciplinarians (Huxley 1998), and reward bad behavior regularly (Dworkin 1997). Children are not pushed to obey guidelines or standards that, even when they do exist, are not enforced (Barakat and Clark 1999).

Permissive parents take orders and instructions from their children, are passive, endow children with power (Gonzalez-Mena 1993; Garbarino and Abramowitz 1992), have low expectations, use minimal discipline, and do not feel responsible for how their children turn out. Ironically, these children turn out to be the unhappiest of all (Neal 2000). They are more likely to exhibit such psychological problems as anxiety and depression (Steinberg 1996), they are the second group (after authoritarian) most likely to commit violence (Steinberg et al. 1994) and engage in antisocial behavior (Simons, Lin, and Gordon 1998). Research links permissive parents with delinquency, substance abuse, and sexual activity (Snyder and Sickmund 2000; Jacobson and Crockett 2000).

In effect, parents teach their children that they can get their way by manipulating others: "Children learn a false sense of control over adults that increases their manipulative behavior" (Huxley 1998). Later on, they do poorly in school, have higher rates of misbehavior in areas involving adult authority, and "may also grow up manipulating around rules because those are not firm" (Thinking n.d.). As they have not been

taught how to control or discipline themselves, they are less likely to develop self-respect. This lack of discipline and structure engenders a desire for some type of control, and so they put "a lot of energy into controlling parents and trying to get parents to control them" (Gonzalez-Mena 1993, 157).

Their unmet psychological needs make them "vulnerable to being easily discouraged by everyday problems and turns the child away from full and satisfying participation in the world" (Garbarino and Abramowilz 1992, 42). This, in turn, hinders their social development, self-esteem, and positive self-concept. Without high expectations to realize, "children of permissive parents generally have difficulty controlling their impulses, are immature, and reluctant to accept responsibility" (Parenting n.d.). Steinberg (1996) shows a strong correlation between permissive parenting and poor grades in families where parents are not involved in their children's education and do not initiate a give-and-take relationship with their children. Other negative outcomes are sleep disturbances (Dworkin 1997) and feelings of insecurity.

Authoritative Parents

Authoritative parenting is high on warmth, moderate on discipline, high in communication, and moderate in expectations of maturity. This style is becoming more pervasive in the West. Authoritative parents are warm and nurturing, create a loving home environment, and provide a high degree of emotional support (Ingersoll 1989). Unlike permissive parents, they are firm, consistent, and fair (Barakat and Clark 1999).

Authoritative parents discipline through rational and issue-oriented strategies in order to promote their children's autonomy while ensuring conformity to group standards (Marion 1999). They establish and enforce behavior standards (Glasgow et al. 1997) and stay in control. "Family rule is democratic [rather] than dictatorial" (Berger 2001, 283). Parents use reason, negotiation, and persuasion-not force-to gain their children's cooperation (Marion 1999). Their listening-demanding ratio is roughly equal. Children are given alternatives, encouraged to decide, and accept responsibility for their actions and decisions. The end result is self-empowerment (Barakat and Clark 1999). When the children's opinions are valued and respected, both children and parents benefit (Marion 1999; Gonzalez-Mena 1993).

Authoritative parents set developmentally appropriate limits and standards for behavior. They make it clear that they will help their children. If their demands are not met, they are forgiving and understanding rather

than punitive (Glasgow et al. 1997; Berger 2000). Overall, this parenting style is high on mutual understanding and based on reciprocity. In fact, both parties benefit. Developmental opportunities are provided for children, as the quality of interaction and nurturance is high and expectations are realistic (Garbarino and Abramowilz 1992). In addition, such parents are more likely to encourage academic success (Glasgow et al. 1997), which has a positive correlation with good grades (Steinberg, 1996). This can be attributed to parental involvement in their children's education and their use of open, give-and-take communication through family reading, writing, and discussions.

Research also shows that these children are less influenced by negative peer pressure and develop successful peer relationships (Collins et al. 2000). As authoritative parenting provides a balance between control and independence, it produces competent, socially responsible, self-assured, and independent children (Gonzalez-Mena 1993). Children are more likely to develop high self-esteem, positive self-concept, greater self-worth, less rebellion, and generally are more successful in life. Furthermore, they are the best adjusted of all children. According to Thinking (n.d.), they ranked highest in self-respect, capacity to conform to authority, and greater interest in the parents' faith in God. They also respect authority, are accountable, and control their impulses. Steinberg (1996) shows that they are more confident and responsible, less likely to use or abuse drugs or alcohol, and less likely to be involved in delinquency. These children also reported less anxiety and depression and the least amount of violence (Steinberg et al. 1994).

Conclusion

Western culture places great importance on planning for children and their upbringing. Hence, parents-to-be spend a great deal of time thinking about everything, from which brand of diapers to use to which college they want their child to attend. However, less importance is given to parenting style. Research has proven repeatedly that parenting styles have a "direct correlation with how children will grow up, how they live and whether they will abide by the rules in society" (Thinking n.d.). Therefore parents-to-be must analyze different parenting styles, their effects, and what works best for them and their child.

References

Barakat, I. S. and J. A. Clark. "Positive Discipline and Child Guidance." 1999. Online at: http://muextension.missouri.edu/xplor/hesguide/humanrel/ gh6119.htm [25.3.2000].

Berger, K. S. *The Developing Person throughout the Lifespan*. 5th ed. New York: 2001.

Collins, A. W. et al. "Contemporary Research on Parenting," *American Psychologist 55*, no. 2 (2000): 218-32.

Daniel, B., S. Wassell, and R. Gilligan. *Child Development for Child Care and Protection Workers*. London: 1999.

Dinwiddie, S. "Setting Limits: Steering down the Rocky Road of Childrearing."KidSource (Feb.l99S). Online at: www.kidsource.com/better.world.press/ setting. limits.html.

Dworkin, P. "Permissive Parenting May Be Hurting Kids' Sleep." *Science Daily Magazine* (9 Oct. 1997). Online at: www.sciencedaily.com/releases/ 1997/10/971009063543.hlm.

Garbarino, J., and R. Abramowitz. "Sociocultural Risk and Opportunity." In *Children and Families in the Social Environment*. Ed. J. Garbarino. New York: 1992.

Glasgow, K. L. et al. "Parenting Styles, Adolescents' Attributions, and Educational Outcomes in Nine Heterogeneous High Schools." *Child Development* 68, no. 3 (1997): 507-29.

Gonzalez-Mena, J. *The Child in the Family and the Community*. New York: 1993.

Gordon, T. *Parent Effectiveness Training*. New York: Plume, 1970.

Huxley, R. "The Four Parenting Styles." Parenting toolbox (27 Sept. 1998), On line at: www.parent-ingtoolbox.com/pstyle1.html.

Ingersoll, G. M. *Adolescents*. Englewood Cliffs: 1989.

Jacobson, K. C., and L. J. Crockett. "Parental Monitoring and Adolescent Adjustment: An Ecological Perspective." *Journal of Research on Adolescence* 10, no. 1 (2000): 65-97.

Marion, M. Guidance of Young Children. 5th ed. Englewood Cliffs: 1999.

Neal, K. Lecture at George Mason Univ. (16 Oct. 2000). "Parenting Styles/Children's Temperaments; The Match."About our kids. Online at: www.aboutourkids.org/parenting/p_ styles.html.

Scarr, S., R. Weinberg, and A. Levine. *Understanding Development*. Orlando: 1986.

Simons, R. L., K. Lin, and L. C. Gordon. "Socialization in the Family of Origin and Male Dating Violence: A Prospective Study." *Journal of Marriage and the Family* 60, no. 2 (1998): 467-78.

Snyder, H. N., and M. Sickmund, "Challenging the Myths. 1999 National Report Series." *Juvenile Justice Bulletin*. Office of Juvenile Justice and Delinquency Prevention (Feb. 2000). Online at: www. ncjrs.org/html/ojjdp/jjbul2000_02_2/contcnts.html [2000, May 25].

Steinberg, L. *Beyond the Classroom: Why School Reform Has Failed and What Parents Need To Do?* New York: 1996.

Steinberg, L. et al. "Over-time Changes in Adjustment and Competence among Adolescents from Authoritative, Authoritarian, Indulgent, and Neglectful Families." *Child Development* 65, no. 3 (1994]: 754-70.

Steinberg, L., and A. Levine. *You and Your Adolescent: A Parent's Guide for Ages 10–20*. New York: 1997.

"Thinking Smart about Parenting." Online at: www.goodliving.virtualave.net.

Resonant Egos and the Art of Married Life

Sermed Öğretim

L ife is an arena where individuals can reveal the secrets hidden in their ego by interacting with the world. Marriage is a part of life that involves the interaction of two egos that are unique in nature. Egos that are resonant with each other produce actions that are also resonant. Conversely, egos which are not in harmony produce actions that eventually lead to the destruction of the marriage. Therefore, to protect the well-being of the marriage, it is vital to achieve resonance between the two egos that make up the couple. This harmony requires an understanding of the ego and a special art in order to harmonize the two egos with each other.

Men and women have different natures that are designed for the duties they are optimized to perform in this life. This difference in natures necessitates different egos as their origin. As witnessed by history, men have an exclusive ego, whereas woman has a rather inclusive ego. In other words, a man's ego leads to a rather self-centered life where communities are composed of distinct individuals, whereas a woman's ego leads to a rather communal life in which the community is considered as the image of one's self. This comparison shows that the properties of ego are very densely packed in every male; this is shown by his individualistic character. So, it is easier to understand the nature and impacts of ego by studying men.

In order to identify the two essential aspects of the ego, consider the following questions: Why are women more likely to go to the doctor if ill, while men drag their feet, refusing to go until it is the final resort? Why are women more likely to ask for directions when they feel lost, while men try as hard as possible not to ask for help? Why do women ask for an expert to fix or assemble something, but men keep working until they are stuck and there is no way out other than calling an expert? Why do men get angry when they are told what they should and how they should do it, both at the same time? These questions reveal the instinct for self-

sufficiency and freedom, which are two essential aspects of the ego. They are very strongly interrelated; so much so that violation of one means violation of the other, or acceptance of one requires acceptance of the other. This relation is explained as follows: Motivated by the instinct of self-sufficiency, the ego does not want to accept its insufficiencies, because an acceptance of insufficiencies requires being open to seeking help from other people; but, receiving help means attachment, hence a violation of freedom. Alternatively, motivated by the instinct of freedom, the ego does not want to accept a power that defines boundaries for its actions because obeying a power means acceptance of weakness, hence insufficiency.

Although men and women are not exactly the same in terms of ego, both of them still carry individuality; and this individuality has the aforementioned instincts. Self-sufficiency and freedom, when used properly, can yield loyal partners that help each other stand together in order to accomplish their life goals. When left untamed and uneducated, self-sufficiency and freedom lead to arrogance, selfishness, and so, a miserable married life. In the long run, uneducated egos become overwhelmed by these instincts and easily break off their relationships with their partners. Therefore, effort must be spent in order to moderate and guide them. Let's ponder over the following example to shed some light on this matter. The forging or shaping of industrial metals requires high temperatures and/or high pressure. If the temperature is high enough to melt the metal, then it can be poured into the mold to give it the desired shape. If the temperature is not high enough, then high pressure is needed to shape the metal; however, the higher the temperature, the lower the pressure required to shape the metal.

Educating the ego means shaping the character of a person; so it involves the shaping of the ego. Similar to the above example, the education of the ego has two main energy sources: heat due to love and pressure due to fear. If the heat of love is enough to melt the ego, then it is very easy to shape the personality. For this reason, most men become a different person when they fall in love. But, if the heat of love is not enough to melt the ego, then the pressure of fear is necessary to make the needed modifications. The source of fear can change from person to person (e.g. fear of God, fear of loneliness, fear of losing dignity, etc.), and fear can manifest itself in another form, which is respect. Whatever the source of the fear is, and however this fear manifests itself, it must be aimed to protect the stability of the relation between the spouses by enabling modifications in the characters as required by the situation.

Use of the fear factor for ego education comes into the picture mostly in later periods of marriages when passionate love has faded and the actual personalities of the individuals are in play. Hence, it is especially in this part of the marriage that an extra effort is required for the successful continuity of the relationship. This effort is called the art of married life. It is an art that reveals the beauties and powers hidden in the hearts; an art that keeps the two instincts of the ego, i.e. self-sufficiency and freedom, under control and guides them. The art of married life involves human specific issues, gender specific issues, and principles needed to maintain mutual harmony.

Human Nature: The Key Points That Are the Same for Both Genders

The Past Life

The past life of a person has an impact on why that person acts the way they do. Therefore, individuals must learn about their partners' life

stories to achieve a mutual understanding. The knowledge of past life has two components: the pre-birth family background, and the atmosphere consisting of the parents, siblings, and friends. The pre-birth family background has to do with the conditions that the baby is born into. The financial, social, and psychological states of the family influence the parents' attitudes towards their child. On top of these states, the parents' past lives compose the unspoken psychological messages given to the child. For this reason, understanding the parents is an important clue to understanding a person. The multi-component atmosphere of the surrounding people determines the conditions under which the innate personality of the person interacts all throughout their life. This interaction instructs the child what the norms and traditions of society are; these in turn motivate and limit the actions of the individual.

As a result of experiences in the past, a person develops a character, which becomes a wall in front of the real nature (innate character) of that person. Therefore, when you are interacting with someone, it is their acquired character that you are dealing with, rather than the innate character from birth. So, it is extremely important to learn about and understand this secondary personality in order to comply with it. The knowledge of the past also makes it easier to have patience in the face of problems and to act compassionately and wisely.

The Innate Character

This is the God-given character or nature of the person. The ego realizes itself in this world through the properties of this character. The individuals who know their innate characters are happy and content in their lives. Success in married life, also, strongly depends on how well the innate character is understood and utilized in the relation. The couples must learn about their own and their partner's innate character and act accordingly in order to achieve a satisfying and happy marriage.

Because of the past life, the innate personality might have been injured and/or suppressed. The spouses at the beginning of their relationship find the loving and accepting atmosphere needed by the innate character to reveal itself and heal its wounds. However, neither the individual nor the partner knows at the beginning how to properly use or guide these newly emerging properties. It takes time to accord them with respect to each other. So, arguments are imminent in this transitional period as a result of mal-adjusted attitudes.

If the innate character is further suppressed, instead of letting it emerge, this can cause deeper psychological and psychosomatic complications in the long run, such as aggressive attitudes towards family members, or deep and extremely long sleep as a form of self-rejection from the situation. Furthermore, the suppression of the innate character can yield uncontrolled psychological messages that are transferred to the children. These hidden messages can have positive or negative effects on the offspring depending on the psychology of the parent. Sometimes they are like underground mines, which produce much that is of benefit as they are uncovered; and sometimes they act like a second subconscious control mechanism for the person that makes up an aggressive and/or distrustful character.

Both the emergence and the suppression of the innate character have potential dangers. However, when treated properly, the emergence of the innate character is beneficial in the long run. The wise way is to try to be patient with each other so that the partners can realize their innate characters and balance them properly to become more contributing members of the family and the society.

Search for the Everlasting Love

Every person has a natural instinct to find an everlasting love that is going to satisfy them in all senses. This instinct is best depicted by the famous expression "live happily ever after"; something that almost never happens: the story always ends at the wedding and the rest is assumed to be irrelevant. Life is full of ups and downs, and no human is ever capable of completely satisfying the heart of another. This is because the heart demands an everlasting love if it is to be satisfied. Therefore, individuals must accept the vast volume of the heart and the limited capability of the human being. This acceptance has two implications: a person should not expect the other partner to completely satisfy their heart, and a person should not try to completely satisfy their partner's heart. A person can at most try to do their best in this way; and as a matter of fact, they must try their best.

Hidden Love Agreement

Every person has a hidden love agreement. This agreement is a sub-conscious list of conditions that form during their past life. If a person was deprived of something that is required by their innate character, then they are going to look for it in their future life. Any behavior that satisfies this need carries the message of love for that person. On the other hand, the innate character of the individual also shapes the ways in which they can receive and give love, hence the language of love. Therefore, the innate character of the person and its interaction with past life experiences determine the content of the hidden love agreement. When an individual feels that they are loved by someone, the hidden love agreement is automatically and subconsciously activated. This means that the other partner is expected to do certain things and behave in certain ways that they are not aware of. Due to lack of awareness of this hidden agreement, both partners may violate the conditions therein. The feelings of being ignored and being dissatisfied with the relationship as a result of these violations lead to conflicts and arguments. As a remedy to the situation, individuals must become aware of the existence of this hidden agreement both for themselves and for their partners, learn about their contents, and act accordingly.

Continuous Development

The ego is like a seed furnished with much potential; and this potential burgeons as time proceeds. Also, past experiences are like seeds that are sown into the soil of sub-conscience; they sprout over time. Some of these sprouts emerge during childhood, whereas some arise during adolescence and still others erupt in maturity and old age. As a result, the person that an individual encounters changes continuously as the relationship progresses. If these sprout-like changes in the personality are not followed and controlled both by the individual and the partner, they are going to grow and exercise their capabilities. These capabilities will require new things to work on and new opportunities to flourish. This situation can lead to dissatisfaction with the current state of the relationship, which may be harmful unless treated patiently.

How Can We Motivate Our Children To Learn?

■ Rahila Bashir

How often do we hear the words "I hate math" or "I don't want to do my homework" and "I don't like school." Just imagine how a caregiver or parent who is concerned and exerts a great deal of time and effort feels when they find the child still refuses to respond positively towards learning. Why is my child not interested in learning? What makes my child not want to go to school? Why does my child say learning is boring? Why is he/she showing higher results in one subject than in another? Why does he/she no longer enjoy English? These are just some of the questions which arise with concerned parents when their children demonstrate a lack of interest in studying both at home or at school. Some parents have opted for home schooling, while others have their children join breakfast clubs, sports clubs or after-school creative clubs as a means to enhance their child's thinking and stimulate interest in them for learning. God Almighty urges us in chapters of the Holy Qur'an to spread knowledge and not to conceal it.

He also speaks of children in numerous verses with regards to their upbringing and welfare. The first verse which was revealed to Prophet Muhammad, peace and blessings be upon him, is *iqra* meaning "read"; this again emphasizes the power of knowledge for a human being to attain success in both worlds. It is narrated by Ibn Masud that, "God's Messenger would take care of us by preaching at a suitable time so that we would not become weary. He abstained from pestering us with religious talk and knowledge all the time[1]." The noble Prophet said, "The pen has been lifted from three: the child until he reaches puberty, the insane until he is cured and the one who is sleeping until he awakens[2]." We are commanded to be mild and loving towards children. Give instructions gently to make things easy. It takes time for the child to understand what one is saying and to respond accordingly and correctly.

---

1   *Sahih Muslim*, 1, 68
2   *Sunan at-Tirmidhi*, Hudud, 1; *Sunan an-Nasa'i*, Hudud, 17

But remember a child is not accountable for their actions so be patient while they respond to you in their own time. Children differ from one another in intelligence and comprehension. Some can be corrected by a mere stern glance and others need to be scolded firmly. But we should never stop following the advice of God's Messenger who said "Those who do not show mercy to our young are not from us[3]." A child is won over with tenderness, mildness, and love. Let us now look at some of the reasons why our children may display a lack of interest in learning. Sometimes the reasons can be obvious; maybe the parents do not have the time to interact with homework tasks and the children struggle without this assistance, or maybe there are far too many distractions in the environment, so the child finds it hard to concentrate. But there can also be hidden pressures; perhaps the child does not like a particular subject, or finds it difficult to understand it, or does not enjoy writing or arithmetic.

Sometimes a change of routine or a new teacher can affect the child, peer pressure or lack of confidence can also result in a lack of interest in studying at school or at home. The important question is how do we, as parents or education workers, draw the child's attention to learning and generate joy and satisfaction in them? The early years of a child's life are of utmost importance and play a crucial role in determining every child's future. Brain research has confirmed that the experiences children un-

3   *Sunan at-Tirmidhi*, Birr, 15

child becomes overwhelmed by a large task. It is not that the task is difficult in itself, but the child may feel nervous, fearful or confused, resulting in a need for more time or input to understand the concept better. A child will sometimes abandon a task they even begin to try, so it is best to help your child break the task down into a series of smaller tasks. Also allow children to set their own weekly targets which they can reward themselves for completing.

4. Help your child learn to arrange time as when they start to go to school some may learn quickly and easily at different levels or stages of learning, but others may not. However later on, they will need to know how to independently set aside time to complete certain tasks.

5. Praise your child's efforts since some children have trouble connecting personal effort to achievement. To help a child succeed, efforts should be praised at every success and the praise should be specific. So rather than saying "you could have done that better," you could say, "you tried your best and worked hard."

6. Help your child take control; underachievers sometimes see achievement as something that is beyond their control and this makes them feel as if all their efforts are pointless. The child needs to understand the role personal responsibility plays through success.

7. Keep a positive attitude about school because children need to see that their parents value education. Even if a child's problems in school are a result of a problem with the schools or the teacher, you need to be careful about what you say and when.

8. Help your child make a connection between their schoolwork and their interests. Sometimes children lack motivation because they cannot make a connection between the work they are being asked to do and their goals and interests. For example, a child who wants to be an astronaut should know that maths and science are important in these jobs. However, under-motivated children generally do not focus on anything but the present. They cannot plan ahead for the near future, so they rarely reflect on adult life or ambitions.

9. Turn homework into games as most children love a challenge, particularly with a familiar person whom they trust. Sometimes, dull homework can be turned into something exciting like a challenging game.

Checking children's work shows them you care about it. Another creative approach to homework is to link it to an interest or encourage them to mark it for themselves.

10. Adults should keep in mind that motivation is not always about school achievement and that it is important to note that some children are highly motivated to achieve goals, even if the goals are unrelated to school. Remember achievement is *not* motivation. It is therefore very important to know that while you may get your child to get the homework done, he or she may never be truly motivated to do it. So what is the difference between the two; what is motivation? Motivation is a temporal and dynamic state that should not be confused with personality or emotion. Motivation is having the desire and the willingness to do something. A motivated person can be aiming at a long-term goal, such as becoming a professional writer, or a more short-term goal like learning how to spell a particular word. Attention from a pupil is necessary and essential for learning and this gives a student a feeling of self worth and makes them want to exert effort.

If a teacher can secure the interest of the pupil and the student does the work assigned, and if the work holds their attention, interest is maintained. There are two kinds of interest, the positive and the negative. When a student has a positive interest in learning, they are getting value because there is something they want to obtain. But if they only have a negative interest, they may still learn a small portion of what is being taught, but not as much as if they were to have a positive interest. The student needs to have a desire of their own to learn and learning should be a result of this, not of outside pressure. They will strive to learn if their interest is positive. If a child is interested in a subject, a wise teacher or parent can make use of this interest. They can work towards maintaining this motivation for learning. But before an adult can hold a child's interest, they need to have an understanding of how the interest is obtained and how purposes that cause an appetite for learning develop in individuals. A person's daily life, their character and their personality all determine their drive for learning. This interest can lead them to take action and want to acquire knowledge. There is also a need for a desire to be active; if a person is lazy, they will not have desires or urges to learn. A student also needs to have a desire for approval from their parents, teachers and peers. They need to have a desire to have a feeling of accomplishment, as this will lead them to seek more and more knowledge. They need to feel proud about their personal accomplishments.

We have not been able to mention all the desires that lead to motivation and learning here, but we have touched upon a few of the primary desires. Some parents may feel they do not know the best way to keep their child motivated with the same joy and satisfaction away from school and at home. Parents can worry over this, but it is comforting to know that a simple activity, such as a trip to the park or library or a small activity such as cooking or planting with your child can be interactive, fun, enjoyable and always a creative part of learning. Talking to your child's teacher or other parents in similar situations is always encouraging and you may pick up tips for new steps that will help bring enthusiasm to your child's education. At the present time we are fortunate to have easy and affordable resources and free websites which help parents to understand this topic better and which provide step-by-step guidelines on how to generate the joy of learning in kids. The curriculum in schools is continuously reviewed and updated to be a friendly and interesting framework of teaching and learning, with interaction between teachers and students across the globe.

The Importance of Maternal Care

■ Dr. Osman Küçükmehmedoğlu

A lmost all animals come into the world without the need of long training or education to manage their lives. Whatever knowledge they need to do so is either "deposited" in their being—modern materialistic science misnames it as *instinct*—or is continually "inspired" in them. However, in this respect, as in so many others, man is completely different from animals. He comes to the world without knowing anything but with a capacity to learn, that is, he comes needing training and education. The more compatible with his disposition the education is, the more attuned to his spiritual, intellectual and material needs, the better and more beneficial and character-building it is. Among all living beings, it is also man who needs the longest period of care and upbringing. Although most modern legal systems have set the age of discretion at 18 years, it may be said that, with rare exceptions, a person does not reach the age of discretion much before 30 years. Almost everyone, even a genius, needs to consult with others before taking important decisions. Besides, everyone is susceptible to making errors and therefore in need of correction. This is

because man is a fallible social being compelled to live together with his fellow men and co-operate with them. The first school where he receives education and learns social manners is his family.

Especially in infancy, man is in dire need of love and affection. For man to grow into a resolute, well-educated, well-mannered and loving, useful member of society, and a strong, sound, healthy individual, the warmth of a family environment is of the greatest importance. In this environment, the mother has a special place. It is the mother who nourishes the infant with her milk. Probably more than her milk, the love, care and affection of the mother for the baby have great significance for the development of sound human personality and character. The first twelve months of the relationship between mother and baby is called the symbiotic period during which the baby feels a deep attachment to its mother. Indeed, in the first six months or so, the baby cannot distinguish its mother as a being separate from itself. It begins to do so only after this period. During this first year of life, the love of the mother forms the foundation of the baby's spiritual personality and develops in it the feeling of self-confidence. The mother's love is also an important factor in the development of the baby's intelligence and in enabling the baby to grow as a social being. Long or short term separation of the mother from the baby gives rise to depressive anxiety.

Dr R. Spitz, a modern psychiatrist, defined two syndromes in children who have grown up without sufficient maternal love. One of these syndromes, called anaclitic depression, arises from short-term separation of the baby from its mother after the first six months. This usually occurs when the baby is placed in a public nursery. The baby thus separated from its mother reacts initially with long, loud cries. If one approaches it when it stops crying, it begins to cry again. After this initial reaction it stops crying and an expression of exhaustion and sulkiness appears on its face. Dr. Spitz called this the period of protest: the baby begins to eat less and lose weight and its physical development ceases. Vomiting and diarrhea may accompany these symptoms. The period of protest, usually two or three weeks, is followed by a period of depression when the baby is sulky and mournful. After two months, these emotional reactions become less frequent. The baby now becomes uninterested in its environment and in those who approach it. In short, it introverts.

The meaning of these phases of response is easily understood. The baby first of all reacts against separation from its mother with long, loud cries to call her back. After that, it grieves. Then, when it is no longer hopeful of reunion with its mother, it suffers depression and becomes introverted. If the separation does not exceed three months, the baby can recover and restore to its former state. But if the separation continues beyond three months, the baby does not recover fully and develops a long-term separation depression. This kind of depression arises in infants separated in very early life and brought up in public nurseries or hospitals for long periods. It is characterized by insufficient bodily, spiritual and intellectual development and growing up as a dissociable being.

A baby has the deepest need for its mother's direct care and close attention especially in the symbiotic period. Even in the most professionally-run nurseries the baby cannot find a substitute for the affection, love and interest its mother can show it. Whereas the baby is embraced by a halo of care and love in the family and attracts the direct attention of its mother, in nurseries it has to share the care of a stranger, however professional or efficient a caregiver he or she may be, with at least ten or fifteen other infants. Whereas it is embraced, caressed, kissed and played with many times in the family, and is in the lap of love, in a public nursery it is abruptly deprived of almost all of these things in an alien environment.

Children separated from their families in the early years of their lives and left in public nurseries suffer difficulties in adapting to new environments and circumstances in later life, and give late responses to different stimulants. They develop tics and other involuntary movements such as swinging their legs while sitting, leaning against something, hitting the head against a wall, pulling their hair, playing with their ear lobes, and shaking the head. Such behavior of an infant left without its mother is in part an attempt to compensate for the loneliness and deprivation it feels. In addition, some sort of mental retardation may be observed in them. Studies have shown that, even in properly and sufficiently nourished children, rates of susceptibility to illness and death are higher. Compared to their equals in age, they are usually less in height and weight. Although thirsty for love, they respond with indifference or suspicion when they are shown love and nearness.

Some of the children deprived in this way grow up destitute of self-confidence; some become timid, reserved and passive, others become aggressive. They display signs of ill-breeding such as petty theft and truancy. Some of them are disposed to criminal behavior and violence. They may also commit suicide or attempt it. Studies done on criminals and the mentally ill have shown that most of them spent their childhood separated from their families, deprived of love. Character weakness and personality defects, which arise as a result of long-term separation from the mother, are unfortunately, long lasting. The younger a baby is when placed in a nursery and the longer it remains there, the more undesirable the effects are.

In sum, the love and care a mother shows her baby is so important for the growth, education and character of the child, that nothing can compensate for the lack of it. The symptoms observed in children growing up separated from their families also appear in adopted children. These children cannot adapt easily to the new family and can never have the same feeling towards their adoptive mothers as they have towards their own mothers. The state of children in divorced families or "broken homes" is still more pathetic.

Why is Internet Control Necessary?

■ Mehmet Köylü

"At school we had difficulty answering questions like Who am I? What do I expect in life? Where will I go? What's the meaning of life? Using drugs... Having meaningless conversations... Listening to foreign pop music and memorizing the lyrics... Living in this music and atmosphere as if it were real. It was the thing most dear to us."

This person also mentioned that the deaths of two of his friends had been covered up. He underlined the fact that they were living in a world of emptiness, away from Europe and isolated within Turkey in the following words:

> *"Our high school was like an island. Children who had everything lacked sincerity and real friendship on this island. We lived a certain jargon, a subculture in this frame of odd estrangement. We weren't yet interested in politics. On the other hand, our school taught us how to think. In English and German classes we discussed the meaning of life after reading Kafka, Camus; but the world our foreign teachers took us to was far away. We weren't living in Europe. We also were completely isolated from Turkish society. If we had been living in Germany, we would have learned individualism, egoism, how to protect our interests from nursery school on. However, everything we wanted was procured immediately, even our breakfast. Our Turkish teachers would enter our classes, however, they were not of the same status as us, and they felt inferior. Foreign teachers would come for a period of 4–5 years and were familiar with neither Turkey nor the Turkish mentality."*

As is evident in these words, some young people read books by writers like Kafka and Albert Camus, books based on existential philosophy. These books tell of how human beings fall in this world and criticize the meaninglessness of life, encouraging young people to think about the values of the community in which they live. This can be a dangerous

thing if a young person does not come from a family with deeply rooted values, or lives in a society where there are no healthy alternatives offered to the traditional values of that society.

These young people are brought up in isolation from the history, culture, national and spiritual values of their society, causing them to rebel against their own identity and personality. Such circumstances push young people, if they lack spiritual support, into a spiritual emptiness and finally into a dead end, where the only way out may be suicide. One of the fundamental reasons for such suicides is that these children are being taught nihilist ideals and are being brought up in an artificial environment, an environment which has been transplanted from the West, but one in which only the outward trappings have been taken, and the roots, i.e. the values, have been left behind. This can in no way be a healthy situation, the environment that these children find themselves in is foreign to the environment of their families and neighborhoods, and is lacking everything. Is it any wonder then that these children end up committing suicide?

Who Is Merely Called a Satanist and Who Is Really a Satanist?

We should be very careful when we talk about Satanism and we should avoid explicitly calling anyone a Satanist. We should follow the precept 'innocent until proven guilty.' Unless a person says that he is a Satanist or decisive proof is brought forward, sorting people into various categories and regarding some young people as Satanists may lead to uneasiness and reaction in society. To put it more simply, any wrong move or action made by officials may cause those who are not Satanists to join them. As mentioned before, Satanism is a reactionary movement. One needs to be very careful.

These issues were discussed in September-October of 1999, when Satanism was high on the agenda and some reactions were voiced, such as, "People should not be categorized according to the music they listen to, the color of their clothes, the style of their hair, or the earrings they wear, and they should not be regarded as Satanist according to such". Indeed, not everyone who listens to rock, metal, or heavy metal music is a Satanist. Similarly, not everyone who wears black T-shirts and jeans is a Satanist. People should be able to decide what clothes they wear for themselves. On the other hand, it should be kept in mind that young people who claim to be Satanists listen to rock and metal music, and prefer black because it represents the "dark powers".

What Should Be Done to Prevent Young People from Falling into the Trap of Satanism?

There is no doubt that the main responsibility for preventing young people from drifting toward Satanism lies with the family. Families play a crucial role in the shaping of a young person; a dysfunctional family may well help in determining whether a young person is inclined toward Satanism or not. We know that young people from broken or dysfunctional families cannot find the essential love, care and support from their families, and thus are in danger of becoming interested in Satanism. Parents should take care of their children as a trust from God and be careful about whom they make friends with, where they go, whether they acquire undesirable habits, what time they get home in the evenings, and whether they attend school regularly. It should be remembered that Satanism spreads in Muslim countries through young people and cliques.

A good friend is also a good example and a bad friend a bad example. Moreover, parents should neither oppress their children, nor should they be too permissive. They should try to be their friend at times, while trying to understand them. They should try to fulfill the wishes of their children, if it is for something legitimate or they should dissuade the child when such a desire is wrong. They should remember that their children need both financial and spiritual support and they should look for ways to spiritually satisfy their children.

Many children today complain that they look for happiness outside their families, mostly in their groups of friends, because they cannot find love, support, and happiness. Finding the love and support that one desires from one's own parents outside the family is impossible, if the parents fail to provide it. It is not enough to provide young people with money. They need love, care, and compassion as much as they need material things. Parents do not do their children any favor if they grant all their wishes, provide them with endless financial means, and leave them free to make their own choices. Parents should know when to say no, restrict certain behavior, and even make children earn their own pocket money. It seems that some young people have tried everything and have everything they want in life, leaving only Satanism; therefore, they want to try this too. What all this goes to show is that youngsters should be brought up in accordance with the realities of life and should learn how to shoulder certain responsibilities. Some families whose children have been trapped by Satanism say that they fulfilled every financial need, but these families never mention what they failed to provide. To put it more clearly, they, for example, begrudge their child, from whom they withhold no material desire, a religious or moral education. The real reason behind the growth of Satanism is a lack of religious education. In addition, certain precautions should be taken, considering the fact that young people who enter such groups are mostly high school students; motives of sex and freedom play an important role in young people joining such groups, and the tendency to prove themselves is especially powerful at these ages.

School principals and teachers can also play an important role in protecting young people from harmful movements like Satanism. They should regard every student as being entrusted to their safekeeping and

should struggle to train them first as a good person and then a good citizen. They should inform the children of harmful movements like Satanism, warn them to stay away from such groups, and help those who have entered them. Educators must have sound information about such subjects in order to teach the students properly. However, they should be very careful when teaching such subjects and avoid making them attractive. Furthermore, the parent-school relationship should be strengthened and students should be prepared for life and future with reciprocal communication.

Officials also play an important role in the proper education of young people to whom we will entrust our future. Governments should not neglect these movements; they should not make the mistake of considering them as marginal. Something should be done even if one individual is lost to Satanism. Moreover, we observe that Satanism spreads rapidly among youngsters and that no serious precautions have been taken. However, Satanism is not the only harmful movement that sweeps up young people. The sinister country of alternative, harmful movements includes those entrapped by Satanism, but at the same time there are the glue-sniffers in dark corners or in subways. We should look after all the young people who have fallen into this dark country and protect

them from all harmful movements; nobody can guarantee that today's glue-sniffer will not become tomorrow's Satanist. Members of the mass media should also take this matter seriously. They should inform people responsibly and with accurate information, sticking to the objective and un-biased principles of journalism. They should not simply regard movements like Satanism as a piece of sensational news, but try to bring forth the real causes that foster the tendency of young people toward such movements. Moreover, they should not ascribe every incident of suicide to Satanism, publicizing the issue by exaggerating it or by putting it on the agenda frequently, making it a matter of curiosity.

On the other hand, parents and all institutions should also attend to the youngsters who have been entrapped by Satanism. They should not cast them out or regard them as dangerous people that belong to an eccentric movement, but rather they should try to help them back to the mainstream. They should also look after those who have been prosecuted and those have served a sentence; most youngsters do not know what Satanism is or how dangerous a path it is. If they had known, they probably would not have tended toward such a movement. If parents sense that their children are interested in such a movement, they should not try to cover it up in shame, but rather they should bring it out into the open, asking for help from those who are familiar with the subject or from a psychologist or psychiatrist. Those who see such a tendency in their friends should also look after them and inform the parents and teachers of their friends immediately. If school principals or teachers feel that their students have such a tendency, they should attend to these children, in cooperation with the family. They should not try to cover up the issue, in the fear that it might harm the school's reputation; nothing is more important than human life.

Research has shown that young people who tend toward Satanism or commit suicide for its sake have little religious faith, having had little or no religious education. This is a reminder of the fact that man is not simply a physical being, but also a spiritual one, a bipolar being. If a person is not spiritually satisfied, they will search for satisfaction in another place, sooner or later, no matter their financial status. This search can sometimes lead down the wrong path; Satanism is the most obvious example.

Unfortunately, the education given in our schools today does not fill this spiritual void. In fact, it is not aimed at doing so. The rapid growth in the number of youngsters who resort to Satanism, drugs, etc. is the most distressing result of this. Similarly, recent research shows that the age for drinking alcohol has dropped to 13, a fact that jeopardizes the future of these young people and consequently of our society. Parents, educators, religious officials, theologians, society, and government officials should fulfill a role in order to fill the spiritual void suffered by young people. Whether one has religious beliefs or not, we should provide our people with religious information. The support our young people need is only available through proper religious education. If we neglect this issue, a spiritual void will emerge. Certain people will exploit this emptiness and the result will be, as in Satanism, that some youngsters will worship in-appropriate objects, and even take on the risk of death for their cause. In fact, Satanism is a phenomenon contrary to human nature, as all mono-theistic religions regard Satan as man's greatest enemy, the representa-tive and promoter of all evil. Satan is neither an object of worship nor does he have a claim for divinity. Moreover, he did not in fact reject God (Ibrahim, 14:22). This is the very reality that lies under the contradiction and inconsistency of Satanism. There is a creature called Satan and some youngsters worship him and accept the risk of death for his sake. This is an anomaly that should be dealt with seriously. If we had informed our young people about God, the Prophet and Satan, nobody would now be worshipping Satan; Satan is a being that should be avoided and stayed away from. However, it is a sad fact that some of our young people worship Satan, man's greatest enemy.

To sum up, let's not categorize our young people according to the music they listen to, the color of their clothes, the length of their hair, or the earrings they wear. At the same time, it is important not to reduce Satanism to certain types of music or certain clothes, hairstyles or accessories. If this were the case, then why and for what cause did these young people die or take their own lives? What is to be done now is not to categorize young people into certain groups with certain names, but rather to look for and produce sound and permanent answers to these two questions: What should we do to prevent young people from being entrapped by Satanism? What should we do for those who are already entrapped? Satanism is not a problem that can be solved by security precautions; it is a matter of acceptance or denial. Several social, psychological, familial, and societal reasons might lie behind young people's drifting toward Satanism, however the real reason for such a tendency toward harmful movements is a lack of religious education and a spiritual void. If a young person regards Satan as a being to be worshipped and dares to commit suicide for his sake, then it is impossible to explain the situation in another way; Satan has become a matter of faith. Immoral behavior that is under the scope of faith can only be corrected with proper religious instruction. We are sorry to say that some families today are paying the price. If we do not want to pay greater penalties, we must attend to our young people; it is to they that we will entrust our future.

References

Barton, Blanche. *The Church of Satan*, USA, 1990, 152–158.

Güç, Ahmet. *Satanizm: Şeytana Tapınmanın Yeni Adı* (Satanism: The New Style of Worshipping Satan), İstanbul, 1999.

Günay, Nasuh. "Şeytana Tapınmada Modern Yol Satanizm" (Satanism, The Modern Way of Worshipping Satan), *Arayışlar*, Isparta, 1999.

Russell, Jeffrey Burton. *Şeytan: Antikiteden İlkel Hristiyanlığa Kötülük* (translation of *The Devil: Perceptions of Evil From Antiquity to Primitive Christianity.* Cornell, 1977), translated by Nuri Plümer, İstanbul 1999.

The Effect of Television in the Early Years

■ Hasan Aydınlı

A mong the greatest inventions of the twentieth century are devices of mass communications. Every invention can have either a positive or a negative effect, depending on how it is used. TV is one of these inventions that are found in the home. The history of family life can be divided into two phases: "before TV" and "after TV." Its effects on the whole family are so immense that they are outside the scope of this article. Instead, we will concentrate on the effects of television on children, and especially on children under the age of 3.

During our interviews with parents, almost all of them had one question: "What is the effect of television on our child?" The importance of this question can be better understood after we have studied the effects of television on our children. The effects of TV depend on how much the children watch TV, their personality, whether they watch alone or with adults, and whether their parents talk to them about what they have watched. Therefore, it would not be true to say that television is absolutely harmful or beneficial. If the necessary precautions are taken, it can be a useful source for both the child's educational and social development, while on the other hand, it can have very harmful and lasting effects on children if not properly monitored and if the child is left to decide when, how much and which TV programs to watch. The effects also vary according to the child's age. This magic box has different effects on children of different age groups. The worst—and unfortunately permanent—effects of television on children occur during the 0–3 age group. This is because some of the psycho-social attributes that are acquired in these years persist in a person's character throughout life. Any problem that originates from this period will affect the rest of a person's life.

The Effects of Television on the 0–3 Age Group

During this period some parents do not (or cannot) spend enough time with their children for a variety of reasons, and they leave their

child alone with the television. Some of the reasons for a lack of time being devoted to the child may be socio-economic factors, the lifestyle of a working mother, problems between the parents themselves, the necessity of housework, parents working additional jobs, a chronic illness in the family, psychiatric problems of the parents, the child being the product of an unwanted pregnancy, the child's physical illness, or dozens of other reasons—all of these can affect family life. Because of these, intentionally or not, some parents often cannot pay enough attention to their child; the only thing they are able to do is to keep up physical maintenance (i.e., feeding the child and keeping him or her clean). In these cases, TV comes in and fulfills the role of the parents, and the child ends up spending too much time in front of the television.

Experiencing full emotional sensations and the complete attention of the parents sets the groundwork in the first three years of life for a strong and healthy psychological make-up. Physical contact, talking to the child, making him or her feel that he or she is loved, playing with the child, spending time with the child all have a positive effect on the development of the psycho-social side of the child. Spending time with a baby prevents him or her from becoming alienated in relationships with other people and helps him or her to recognize the social environment, starting with the parents. Along with this relationship, a close tie between the child and the mother develops. This relationship starts in the mother's womb and continues during infancy. The child begins to be able to communicate and express his or her needs. As time goes on, the child starts to be able to establish a dialog with other people.

Since the basic foundation of communication is speech, children have to learn how to talk. In order to be loved by people, they have to understand people and respond to emotional stimulation. Children need encouragement in order to socialize and develop communication, especially from those who are in charge of the upbringing. This encouragement and approval, attention to the child's needs (food, clothing, hygiene, safety, etc), paying attention to the child's problems, spending time with the child, kissing, caressing, talking and playing with the child all go towards helping the child feel that he or she is loved; these constitute an encouragement for the bio-psycho-social development of the child.

The reason we mention all these is so that we can better understand the television-child relationship. When the child is left for a long time in front of a device that does not respond to his or her words, looks and smiles—a device devoid of sensual and social stimulants, without emotion—and when the child is deprived of physical closeness to the person with whom he or she has established close ties, problems will occur as time passes. Although television provides sounds and images, the child is not yet of an age to interpret, accept and benefit from these. The problems developed here will appear later in the form of an incompleteness or inadequateness in the socialization, individualization and the psycho-social aspects of this person.

Why is TV more harmful for children? The child will not have friends or a social environment to make up for the social and sensual incompleteness mentioned above. He or she does not play a role in an interchange, and the child does not have a chance to contribute. Psycho-motor and psycho-social sufficiency has not had a chance to develop and he or she does not have an alternative environment in which to develop. If a child is less than 3 years old and stays too long (the length of time changes from child to child, but generally for more than an hour) in front of a television, and particularly if the parents have any of the problems mentioned above that prevent them from spending more time with the child, then some insufficiency and delay can be witnessed in the child's psycho-social functions. These functions are those that are necessary for the development of social improvement (sensual interaction and responsiveness, adaptation to the social environment, taking an interest in people, showing sympathy to others, paying attention to other children of the same age, etc) and communication (talking, meaningful gestures and mimicry, spelling out words by syllables, perception, making sounds, forming sentences, etc). If such conditions occur, a child psychiatric must also investigate what other reasons may have caused such conditions. The replacement of time that should be spent with other people with time spent before the television has very serious drawbacks.

If children stay in front of the television too long during this period, some psychiatric abnormalities may develop. The child may show symptoms of indifference to his or her surrounding, for example, he or she may not look around when called, the child may avoid making eye con-

tact, or show indifference to other people and children of the same age, the child may experience difficulties in taking part in emotional or social communication, he or she may try to stay on his or her own, or may display repetitive behavior, like turning around or rocking back and forth, the child may become obsessed with objects, he or she may be slow to speak and construct sentences, or may display problems in establishing dialogue, or the child may be unable to respond sentimentally. Therefore, in order to prevent excesses, it would be appropriate for the parents to put a limit on television for the benefit of normal psycho-motor and psycho-social development in the child.

At the same time, it would be appropriate for both the father and the mother to spend as much time as possible out of their normal daily life with the child, playing with him or her, speaking to the child, showing the child that he or she is loved, showing an affinity with him or her, taking the child out, paying attention to his or her physical needs, paying attention to his or her normal growth stages, laying the ground for communication with other children, sparing some time only to be with the child, telling him or her stories. In short, parents do not have to ban television watching completely for their children, but the appropriate thing for the good of the child is to restrict and balance it with other activities.

How to Make Our Children Love Reading

■ Harun Avcı

When reading is mentioned, we usually talk about the reading habits of adults and ignore that of our children. However, if children do not read, and/or if their parents do not read to them, then there is a serious problem. Making children love reading and making them read the right books at the right age is the duty of all parents.

Pre-school Children and Reading

Reading books to little children is one of the best ways of spending time with them. What we tell them at this period has a greater influence on them because this is the period when their personalities are developing. It is a very remarkable fact that Prophet Muhammad, peace and blessings be upon him, counseled Muslims to whisper the *adhan* and *iqama* in a baby's ear as soon as he/she was born. From this we can infer that we should start talking to our child from the very first day. Today, researchers who study child development have reached the same conclusion.

As soon as our baby can differentiate colors and shapes, we can begin to communicate with him/her using books. A picture will catch a child's attention. It is better to explain something to a child with a picture or a photograph, for it is recognized that learning is more effective with visual support. Our child will be interested in books at an early age if we show them the pictures in a book and talk about them. Such a practice is useful in terms of language development and establishing a dialogue between parents and their children, as well as making children feel that their parents love them. A further benefit in introducing books to children at an early age is that it raises their interest in books. In time, books become their close friends and reading becomes a need for them. As Victor Hugo stated, the need to read is like gunpowder, once it is ignited it does not die out.

During the pre-school period, if the parents read books to their children every day, their child's vocabulary will become enriched and their ability to think will improve along with their intellectual progress. In

this way, children will learn to listen and to speak. They will grow up as individuals who love reading. They often ask questions when a story is being read, for children learn by asking. They should be given logical and satisfactory answers. Their questions should never be ignored or undermined. They should never be misinformed. Children are never bored by listening to the same stories over and over again. This helps them to become familiar with the vocabulary and facilitates absorbing the message given in the book.

What Is the Benefit of Books?

Books are the most important means of educating children. We transfer our culture to new generations via books. Books improve language use and teach about life. Children can get to know people through books and evaluate them. Within the plots of novels and stories, children come to recognize human behavior. Starting from this point, they learn what kind of people should be considered as friends and what type of behavior is to be avoided.

A child who reads about the problems in life and the ways to cope with these knows what to do when he/she encounters similar problems in real life. Books teach children to use their imagination and to love people, nature and living things. Books raise interest in inventions and technology. They teach about man's place and his duty in the universe. The stories children read teach them that they should not step on ants, destroy bird-nests, that they should not let animals starve and so on. They make children feel in their consciences that lying, stealing, and fighting are all wrong. Children internalize values, such as being kind to people, helping them without expecting anything in return, courage, determination, modesty, being resolute and striving for success when identifying themselves with the heroes in the books they read. Books are a means of entertainment as well. Riddles, puzzles, mind games and anecdotes contribute to the mental development of children and help them enjoy themselves.

The Reason for Reading

Reading is related to the way we perceive the world and our perspective of life, universe and our self-opinion. Reading is the outcome of the urge to discover new things and our desire, as a human being to understand ourselves, the reason for our existence, our Creator and the mysteries of the universe. This must be the reason why the first order of the Qur'an is "Read". People can achieve these only by reading. So the very question raised is: how can we motivate children toward books and reading?

There is no magical way to make children love reading. Nevertheless, we can try different ways to approach this problem. We have already mentioned some methods that can be used with pre-school children. We can apply different methods for older children. First of all, if the adults at home constantly read and share their opinions with each other about the themes or characters in the books they are reading, the children will develop an interest in reading. Reading starts with the family. Even a little child who cannot read or write holds a book, turns its pages, looks at its pictures, asks questions about it and in the end, reading becomes as natural for him/her as eating and drinking. In short, if reading has a place in our own life, our children will read too.

We should not just present books as a means of transferring information. We should emphasize the entertaining and attractive sides of books also. Children should be made to meet books as if they were meeting a friend. Illustrated story books, novels, books of riddles, puzzles and

anecdotes are usually more interesting for children. Such books warm children to reading. We should read together with our child. Children love this. We should alter the tone of our voice when we read what different characters are saying, trying to animate the story. If the parent is the only one reading, it will be boring for the child. Sometimes the child should read to his/her parents. Some parents habitually read stories to their children before they go to sleep. This is a good method that can be used in most families. Children should be taken to book fairs and bookshops, they should be given time to take a look at the books. They should be allowed to choose some of the books they are to read. We should be careful about choosing books suitable to their age. A book should have interesting illustrations and should be written in a language that is grammatically accurate, yet interesting.

In conclusion, if we choose the right ways, any child can love reading. However, we cannot make a child read a book by force. Even if we cannot help the children to love books, then at least we should not make them hate books. Once a person hates books, it is very difficult for them to warm up to them again.

Career and Kids: Can I Have Both?

■ Safiye Arslan

I was just sitting there hysterically crying and thinking what I would do now. It didn't seem like a right time to have another baby in that point of my life. We had planned so many experiments with my boss just a couple of days ago when we had a research planning meeting together. There were too many things to do, new responsibilities and commitments to keep; however, I was pregnant. My conscience was telling me that I need to cherish this baby since every baby is a miracle and a blessing and God does things for a reason, but I did not want to listen to it. Instead I was trying to decide how and when I should talk to my boss about this pregnancy. He hired me two years ago expecting me to work 60–70 hours per week like all other distinguished researchers in the life sciences. However, my productivity had been affected due to my first pregnancy, which was very problematic. I had morning sickness for five months and I was not even able to keep down water. Since I was dehydrated all the time, I could not go to work most of the days of the week. Unfortunately, things did not get better after I gave birth because my baby was not sleeping at all during the night. Therefore, I had trouble waking up in the morning and struggled with daytime at work. My boss was nice to me and kept telling me I would do better when my child becomes one year old during all these difficult times. Since then I had been doing better and we made plans for more intense research. I was very excited to be able to fully pursue my research and to show my boss how dedicated I was. But I was pregnant again.

I could not talk to him for awhile, because I was worried about disappointing him. However, it was not fair not to tell him as soon as possible. In a few months I would need some time off and he would need some time to find a new person to replace me. I was aware of the fact that he actually would not be able to lay me off because of my pregnancy. He would not act against the Pregnancy Discrimination Act. According to this amendment women affected by pregnancy or related conditions must be treated in the same manner as other applicants or employees with similar abilities or

limitations. In academia, on the other hand, there is a high risk of getting scooped by a competitor if you delay publishing and that's why scholars are pressured to publish new work quickly. The saying "publish or perish" is well-known in academia; therefore, my boss would need to find some-body who will be able to work significantly more hours than I can work. It was not ethical to delay telling him anymore even if I did not want to quit and knew that when I want to go back to work, it will not be so easy to find a job. I was also aware of the fact that in scientific research, if I slow down and take a couple years off, I am done. It is not good enough to have a PhD degree to set me apart from my competitors on the job market. I am expect-ed to get high-quality publications out to apply for a tenure-track faculty position. I need to constantly be an active and productive researcher.

***

At last, I talked to my boss. He was very rational. He asked me if I could manage doing research and raising two kids because research was never meant to be an 8 am to 5:30 pm job. It was not a simple question to answer. I knew that with kids, no matter where I am or what job I have, my life will be challenging. To keep both a family and an academic career intact I need discipline, planning, and some help at work and home. I won't have time for chatting with colleagues, talking on the phone with friends, reading e-mails or taking lunch breaks at work. I will make long to-do lists and pri-oritize each item, and if I can't get all of them done, I will not stress myself out. Instead, I will be happy with the things I have accomplished. Further-more, balancing career and family life is a team effort so I need to share parenting duties with my husband, who is also overwhelmed at work. The most difficult part is that I have to deal with the guilt associated with leav-ing my children to go to work every day. I love them with all my heart and it is so hard to see them crying behind me when I leave them for work.

The actual question was if I really want to go through all this trouble. I began to think about my motivation for my academic career. Many years ago, as a young woman who was trying to find a direction for my life, I had heard about a Turkish Muslim scholar, Fethullah Gülen. As I studied his teachings more, my perception on the roles of women in society had changed. I realized that I can take on many roles besides being a wife and a mother. My conclusion from his teachings was that men or women, every single human being, should serve God, and that serving humanity is serving God since it is done for the sake of His love. Then I thought that doing science, especially studying biochemistry, would be a great way to serve humanity. By the Divine grace of God and with the help of biochemistry, I might prevent the spread of diseases, find cures for them, enhance the nutritional value of crops or even improve plant resistance against environmental stresses, and thus help so many people around the world.

Furthermore, the first word revealed in the Quran was *iqra* meaning "read" (al-Alaq, 96:1) followed by:

> In and with the name of your Lord, Who created—Created human from a clot clinging (to the wall of the womb). Read, and your Lord is the All-Munificent, Who has taught (human) by the pen, Taught human what he did not know.

Iqra is a command to read the signs the Creator placed in creation. So, for me, biochemistry is not only the study of the chemical processes that happen in living things but also a way to better understand God's Mercy, Wisdom, and Power. When I look at a tiny cell under a microscope, or study its biology in a book, I am fascinated by its perfect structure created in such a small size. This little thing controls so many complicated biological pathways at the same time without messing them up. Then, I ask myself who makes cells from nothing and inspires each one to do all those complex functions. The creation of the little cells, the delicate balances in all the cellular pathways, the nutrients and minerals provided to maintain their lives etc. allow me to better understand God's eternal wisdom, power and mercy. Furthermore, the Prophet Muhammad, peace and blessings be upon him, has said: "Seeking knowledge is mandatory for every Muslim (male and female)" and "Whoever takes a path for knowledge, Allah will make an easy way for him or her to paradise." In brief, knowledge and science are my vehicles that can take me to God and heaven. When I re-thought all the reasons why I got into this field, I decided to continue on my journey as a scientific researcher, but this time with some "obstacles".

After 2 months of thinking, planning and contemplating, I told my boss that I would do as much as I can to be a successful scientist and a mother. Afterwards, I even started enjoying my pregnancy and being a mother for the second time. I found comfort and inspiration from a saying of the Prophet Muhammad, peace and blessings be upon him:

"Heaven lies under the feet of mothers." This means a lot to me. I am so happy that all the hard work I do as a mother to raise my kids to become good individuals will be awarded in the hereafter by God. So, motherhood was an opportunity and an honor God has given me, not a burden. I said to myself that as millions of other working women, I will face many difficulties, but this should not prevent me from celebrating every milestone in this pregnancy and afterwards. I would try my best to be a mother like the one in Gracie Harmon's memorable quote: "My mom is a never ending song in my heart of comfort, happiness, and being. I may sometimes forget the words but I always remember the tune." I may not prepare dinners like the ones in cooking shows for my kids; I may not do it all and do it well all the time; but I can still be a mother who provides the most care, love, and compassion for her kids. In addition, no matter how tired I am after a long and busy day, if my two little angels greet me with hugs and kisses that will make me happy. They will cheer me up at home so that I will forget all the problems and stress at work. Besides, it will be wonderful and so much fun to explore their world which is so innocent, lovely and full of joy. I am so blessed to have these tiny, cute and adorable creatures around me.

Going through all of this and reading a lot on this subject have helped me realize a few things. First of all, there is no convenient time for me to have babies in academia. It is a dilemma whether pregnancy is more reasonable during graduate school even with dissertation writing and teaching than it is when I am on the job market or have a tenure-track job or a postdoctoral research position. Second, I need a lot of support and encouragement to maintain my motivation. I need my husband's help to overcome the challenges of managing a family and an academic career. He can't do anything about 5 months of morning sickness and another full year of nursing and sleep deprivation, but he can share parenting responsibilities and household chores. Third, according to a study done by Virginia Valian, who is a distinctive professor of psychology at Hunter College, females are only 13% of all the full professors at universities and 21% at colleges; therefore, more universities started to promote their female faculty's research programs in the science and engineering departments to ensure that more women are walking the halls of academia. For example, Brown University and the University of Rhode Island got $3.3 and $3.5 million grants respectively from the National Science Foundation in 2007 to develop the careers of women in science and engineering departments, where they are significantly underrepresented. There is also a Women Faculty Mentoring Program at the University of Wisconsin-Madison which seeks to support and retain women assistant professors throughout the tenure process. These kinds of programs, which provide funding for principal investigators with their own research projects, or for the inclusion of female researchers, are exciting opportunities and show the support of society and the academic community for women and mothers. This highly encourages me to pursue research and helps me know that I am not alone.

As a result, I am happy with my choice about being a mother and an academic even though it is tough and stressful. I did not deliver my baby, who was a beautiful gift from heaven, on Friday and go to work on Monday. I took a month off after the delivery, so my research halted for a month; however, I am back now. Am I ever going to get a tenure-track job and get tenure? Am I going to be my little ones' unforgettable tune? Simply, I do not know, but I sure hope so.

Games and Toys

■ M. A. Şahin

Games, sports and play with toys are an important part of a fully rounded program of education. We hope for the day when educational psychologists and other professionals in the field who believe in the reality of God and affirm the life of the spirit will deal properly and sincerely with this aspect of education. In the meantime, we allow ourselves to reflect briefly upon some general principles and some particular suggestions.

First of all, games and toys must help children to broaden their minds and become familiar with present and emerging technology. Thus, with some reservations, we would commend model and toy trains, planes, ships, robots and the like. Secondly, in order to develop an aesthetic sense and a taste for art, children may be encouraged to play at decorat-

ing walls, doors and windows, designing book covers, arranging flowers and laying out gardens, etc. Thirdly, children should be encouraged to use toys and play games that develop their design and constructive capabilities. Blocks of diverse sizes, shapes and colors, as well as other building toys' for making houses, garages, bridges and the like, can be strongly recommended.

In later childhood and early youth, children will begin to ask for toys and amusements of different kinds. It is important for a responsible guardian to develop a taste in the young for games appropriate to their age. The games we have in mind can be roughly divided into two groups:

1. Those aiming at developing the aesthetic sense and constructive powers (For examples, see above);

2. Those that train physical abilities and promote development of the body. Examples of the latter are sports such as running, swimming, riding, wrestling, archery, fencing and the so-called "martial arts" (judo and karate are the best known).

Each of these sports (and other similar ones, according to the needs of the time and place) should be encouraged as they come within the circle of the permitted (halal) and are very effective in developing discipline and strength, balance and grace. Their value as entertainment and pastime is, as it were, an additional bonus. In adolescents, sports involving physical exertion and concentration help their bodily development and channel their energies. Older people can also benefit from such exercise which can prevent many of the ailments that arise from prolonged physical inactivity.

Among games and sports, archery, riding, swimming, and running merit special emphasis. They teach poise and confidence on land, water and air, qualities vital to the leaders and enterprising spirits every nation needs for its survival and prosperity. Although in our tradition the martial arts receive little mention, they can certainly be recommended insofar as they do not contradict our moral principles and do not entail unacceptable risk of injury.

Other games and sports might also be commended so long as they do not lead children to waste time or open ways to them to commit sins. Games that involve gambling or betting are of course forbidden and can

on no account be advised either for children or adults. However, we may note in passing, following the opinion of Imam Shafi'i, that chess is permissible unless played for money. Children who have a bent for that kind of mental activity could therefore be directed towards chess, until they reach adolescence.

Any kind of play or entertainment which counters or debases our ethics is unacceptable for both children and adults. Also, sounds and images, instruments and melodies, which arouse evil and lustful sentiments and so corrupt the soul are absolutely forbidden. It is unreasonable, and unkindness to the young, to open the doors for them to forbidden entertainments while those within the circle of the permitted are quite satisfactory. The principal concern of education generally and, therefore, the principal concern of games and sports also, is to provide children with noble feelings and to keep them healthy spiritually as well as physically. It hardly needs saying that forbidden games and entertainments are not intended to raise children to humanity or to ennoble their feelings; rather, it is often the case that they have a negative, corrupting effect on their minds and spirits,

In sum, there is a need for moral awareness and guidance in the choice of entertainment, sports, games, and toys, just as in other elements of the education of the young. Failure to seek and provide such guidance will mean—instead of the healthy, balanced, morally sound and contented adults we desire to make of the young—exposing them to emotional and spiritual damage, with all the evil consequences for social life that follow therefrom.

The Importance of Breast-Feeding

■ Dr. H. Nurbaki

Mothers shall suckle children for two whole years, for those who desire to complete the suckling. It is for the father to provide for them and clothe them honorably. No soul is charged save to its capacity: no woman should suffer because of her child, nor any man because of his. The same responsibilities are incumbent on the heir. But if (the couple) decide by mutual consent to wean (the child), there is no blame on them. And if you desire to seek nursing for your children (by hiring a foster mother), there is no blame on you provided you pay her fairly. Fear God, and know that God sees everything you do. (al-Baqarah 2:205)

Breast-feeding is extremely important for the mother's own health, as well as that of her baby. The propaganda in the sixties and seventies of some materialistic physicians in cahoots with baby-food manufacturers tried to throw doubt on the value of breast-feeding and to present it, especially in "Third World" countries, as something second-best, unsophisticated. More recently, however, the scientific community has been forced to recognize the irreplaceable value of the mother's milk, compared to any artificial product, and the World Health Organization has banned all negative propaganda directed against it. In what follows, I shall try to answer, from a scientific standpoint, these three questions:

a) What does mother's milk impart to the baby?
b) What should be the frequency and duration of nursing?
c) What effect does nursing have on the mother?

The Nature of Mother's Milk

For nourishment human beings need the three basic foods, and phosphorous and vitamins. All of these substances, namely proteins, sugar, fats, phosphorous and vitamins, are present in the mother's milk. The special worth of breast milk, however, lies rather in the fact that it contains these substances in very subtly tuned proportions, and the most important secret of its composition is that fatty molecules are dispersed within it in very fine, small particles.

The mother's own breast milk is prepared more richly than the table of a tycoon. To begin with, the entire vitamin requirement of the baby is present in it for the first six months. Properly informed science can only be amused at the sight of over-anxious parents rushing about with a fruit press in their hands in an effort to provide baby with Vitamin C.

Secondly, there are antibodies in the mother's milk during the first six months that protect the baby against all infectious diseases. There are even antibodies protecting against measles in the milk of a mother who has never contracted measles, an inexplicable fact in biological terms. This can only be a Divine indication of the value God places on the well-being of His creatures. Certain atheistic scientists have put forward an absurd claim that breast milk is deficient in iron. It has been established in recent years, however, that in adults blood is produced in the bone marrow, whereas in babies it is produced in the liver. Iron is stored in

the baby's liver even while it is in the mother's womb. Attempts to compensate for this supposed deficiency by medicines containing iron may condemn babies to a lifetime of enteritis.

It is a biological imperative that the baby be nursed on breast milk during the first six months, since the liver, normally the centre of digestive activities, is largely occupied with blood production in babies. Furthermore, the baby uses nutrition for the purposes of growth and development rather than energy. For this reason, it is next to impossible to select and balance the required food types and vitamins. We know that there are more than 50 vitamins in addition to the handful known to medicine. The growth and development of the baby is, through the perfect balance of breast milk, brought under perfect control by Divine Omnipotence. To attempt to imitate this Divinely managed blessing with imperfect human imitations of it is both arrogant and ridiculous.

Intervals and Duration of Breast Feeding

Another burden atheists have put on breast-feeding is the rule of feeding every four hours, which they have invented by analogy with the normal period of digestion. Recent research has shown that milk is completely digested in 45 minutes. When this period is over, the secretion of milk in the mother's mummeries increases by a telepathic reflex, and the baby normally begins to cry due to hunger. All these events constitute a biological computer system, and if the feeding periods do not correspond, the baby's stomach is filled with acid, seriously disrupting its digestive system. It has even been conjectured that this may contribute to ulcers in later life. Regarding the duration of breast-feeding, modem medicine has imposed a wholly arbitrary period, namely nine months. But the basic logic of suckling is based on two facts:

a) The liver is heavily loaded because it is producing blood, and hence there is a need for milk. It takes about two full years for the liver to recede into the background as regards blood production. For this reason, breast-feeding should last two years.

b) The most important phase of development, the period when basic biological materials are required, is again two years. Medical science definitely recognizes that the first two years of development of the baby are the most significant phase.

Another miracle of the Qur'an's wisdom is that it specified this period, although, before Islam, the practice in societies in the Middle East was to breast-feed for four to five years.

A final point in regard to the length of the breast-feeding period is that research on childhood mental disorders has shown that an infant needs to be breast-fed for about two years for mental health to be robust. A study done on a global scale revealed that no child in Indonesia and the Philippines suffered mental problems, and the research committee found that this was due to the sense of security and tenderness imparted to the baby during two years of breast- feeding in those countries.

The Benefits for the Mother

a) The healthy functioning of the mammary glands

Health statistics gathered worldwide have shown that breast cancer occurs seldom in mothers who breast-feed their infants for one or two years. Mothers who do not do so, on the other hand, run the greatest risk of contracting this disease. If only for this reason, a one or two-year nursing period should be commended as a cancer preventive.

b) Biological regeneration occurring in the mother's body during nursing

The liver functions at full capacity in a mother who breast-feeds. All the chemical problems of the mother's body come under scrutiny in this way. Further, since all the required substances have to be mixed into the maternal blood, the mother's cells compensate for their deficiencies during nursing. Again, since the pituitary gland is in full control during nursing, the general hormone processes all function properly, and hence the psychological makeup of the mother is vastly improved. This harmony in the hormone balance of nursing mothers and the period of calm it imposes on the psychological structure is a priceless gift. You may have noted that despite being physically tired, nursing mothers are never ill-tempered. The reason for this is the harmonization of glandular secretions during breast-feeding.

Again thanks to this hormonal balance, the womb and ovaries of the nursing mother are also afforded a period of rest. Although this period is not equal to the nursing period, repose of two to six months is a very valuable rest in terms of the mother's sex organs. In the meantime, simple disorders of the womb and ovaries are also cured. Two years is, again, the ideal duration of the nursing period for these benefits to fully manifest themselves.

In sum, the disparagement of mother's milk and of breast feeding generally by proponents of an atheistic modern medicine must rank as one of the most shameful stains on the history of medicine. Biologically and psychologically, the health of both mother and baby is greatly improved by breast feeding for, ideally, up to two years. Independent scientific studies have confirmed that this is so. We should not be surprised that they have done so. For who would know better what is best for the well-being of mankind than the One who created us?

Children and Violent Computer Games

■ Hasan Aydınlı

Suddenly he got up from where he was sitting and started to shout. He was furious just because he couldn't kill the man who was firing at him. He sat down and tried again. He was hopping mad just to get rid of the man opposite him. He gave great damages to his rival. When the man opposite him was lying in a pool of blood, he mercilessly laughed. He repeated all these actions again and again. He was violently fighting and was trying all he can to harm his enemies. Although his mother called him a few times for dinner, he didn't move from his desk. He was so much plunged into the game that he was not able to think of anything else.

Such scenes are very common now in many households and Internet cafes. Children and youth are spending most of their times playing computer games. While parents favor computers as necessities of modern age and as assistants for their children's homework, children mostly consider them as toy boxes. They initially start with innocent intentions, but in time they lose their original purpose. "Uncontrolled use of computers," the common problem of many parents, is also a matter very difficult to solve for the experts. How do computer games affect the children's subconscious and their future lives? Do games with positive effects have an appealing presentation?

Computer games can be grouped under two categories:

- the games that help developing talents, understanding the life experiments and ethical values by using an entertaining method

- the games that do not contribute anything to the child's imagination and thinking abilities and inciting violent and immoral behavior

For the game to positively affect the child's intellectual, physical and spiritual development depends upon both the content and the duration of the game. This period of playing time should neither be too short, nor too long. To be able to obtain a proper balance in this matter, we should first equip the child with an education of using time wisely. Children wasting their time for useless activities can also be insensitive to effec-

tive use of time when they grow up. Concisely, children must acquire the consciousness of valuing time. Wasting time in front of computers cause children and youth to get passive. This increases the stress experienced by the children. Especially in active boys, this inactiveness causes an energy accumulation which negatively affects the child's behaviors. The use of excessive energy by ways of different sports is very useful for the physical and mental development and raising of a social conscience. Moreover, spending time in front of computers deprives children and youth from cultural activities like playing group games, studying together and engaging with a sports activity.

Many of us complain that our children cannot express themselves properly and are not clear at communicating with their environment. When we ask a question to our child, we either get a very brief or a routine answer. Times elapsed aimlessly in front of computers have a significant effect on this.

We see that violence increase in each level of any new computer game. The game producers consider every type of method as permissible just to be able to attract children to the screen. Scenes which are not suitable for the age form the subconscious of a child. Children who have been exposed to several violent scenes are mostly inclined to aggression, anxiety and panic and they are generally furious and quick-tempered and consider violence as an ordinary matter. Reactions of children who watch violent films and play fierce and crimson computer games change in time and start applying more and more force to people and children around them. They tend to hit and kick others even after a slight disagreement. Being affected from destructive violent scenes, children reveal problems like over anxiety, sleep disturbances and behavioral disorders. Since the causes and effects of behaviors affected by the five senses are not questioned so much in pre-school children, abnormalities mentioned earlier can be seen more on them. We can give these as example: "A three-year-old child, who watched violent films, applied what he watched on TV and stabbed and killed his little brother with a knife. Another child who thought himself to be a Pokémon (a cartoon character), threw himself from the seventh floor with the intention of flying. And another child in France who could not win any computer games became epileptic because of having too frequent and excessive anger fits due to the unsuccessful playing sessions." Unfortunately we often hear such news. In order to illuminate the subconscious

of our children with beauties, favors, affection, and altruism, we should offer them alternative, useful and educational games.

Harmful games also prevent children to learn their own culture, thus cause a cultural corrosion. Such games take our children to a world of weird clothes and hairstyles, weapons being the accessories. In this virtual world, no values exist except for "might is right". Furthermore, in most of these games, Islam is shown as a "boogeyman" and Muslims are shown as terrorists deserved to be killed. Children who are seized by computer games become alienated in their environment. Having difficulty making friends around them, children become enslaved by the computer and isolate themselves from society. The only friend of the child is the computer, and in spite of elapsing the time, the child still feels great loneliness inside. Hence, parents should provide suitable activities for their children and reasonably arrange the time spent for computer games.

Many bad characters shown on computer games also have perverse effects upon the child's personal development. It is definite that messages given by these games like being strong and unchallengeable, inconsideration of other people's lives, killing for the sake of living, disdaining ethical values, despising other people's feelings, disrespecting the person addressed, categorizing the people, negatively affect the child's personal development. Such games also impose unfavorable impacts upon learning abilities and awareness of the child. Scenes that are rapidly changing on computer screen distract the child greatly, make him confused and disturb his mind. This triggers a difficulty in concentration when learning. Furthermore, excessive light changes may cause epileptic fits for some children.

Conclusively, computer games inspire children that life is only a game and lead them to think too much about the characters in the game, and mentally and physically to be with them all the time. Children playing too much computer games carry the same concepts of the game into their relations with their family and friends, cause them to confuse the difference between reality and imagination, and eventually, the time spent together decreases and unsocial behaviors settle in the child's personality.

Surely, we cannot underestimate the beneficial sides of the computer which is a must in modern age. But the question is to benefit from the positive services of the computer and to ensure a protection against its harmful usage. The playing time which is essential for the child's healthy growth, should be distributed fairly between virtual games and real group games. For this, we must prefer games which:

• they can play an active role,
• are suggested by specialists and other experts,
• can provide national awareness and cultural identity,
• support comprehension and intelligence of the child,
• contribute to virtues like sharing, team spirit, caring for others, honesty, and diligence,
• instigate curiosity and make learning fun,
• include parents into the game,
• infuse consciousness of performing duties and responsibility,
• help developing imagination, thinking ability, exploring and inventing capability.

If eyes, ears and other organs that are bestowed upon us by the All-Compassionate Creator are engaged with only entertaining computer games, then they are being used out of their innate purposes. Therefore, the vital responsibility of parents is to be very careful for guiding their children to use their sight, hearing, feeling, judging faculties in the right direction and to prepare an environment that provides the child a rich learning background and to bloom his mental abilities.

Satanism and Youth's Quest for Identity

■ Ahmet Güç

B riefly defined as the worship of Satan as if he were God, Satanism is the name given to a reaction that basically started in the 1880s in such countries as France, England, Germany, and particularly in the US, against Christianity and religious understanding and the domination Christian scholars exercised from the Middle Ages onwards. The movement began to be systematized in the 1950's by the American-born Anton Szandor LaVey. Today, Satanism represents a rebellion against all religions "mainly Christianity" and the sacred values that they put forward. Thus Satanism, taking on the nature of Satan's most important characteristic, i.e. opposition and rebellion, is opposed to religion and everything religious, and is for Satan and everything that he represents.

Derived mainly from the witchcraft practices of Europe in the Middle Ages, Satanism has also been seen to be on the rise in Muslim countries. It has become a problem that now appears frequently on the agenda in Muslim countries, as it has begun to attract young people as a rebellious alternative to the philosophy and lifestyle of their parents. Brought to the attention of the Turkish nation when two students at Alman Lisesi (German High School), Aslı and Alp, committed suicide in Ataköy, İstanbul, June 22, 1998, Satanism tends to find a place among high school students. Moreover, it has been reported that Satanism has spread among students at private schools and has even become popular with primary school students.

Research reveals that young people involved in Satanism share common characteristics. For example, they are mostly children of well-to-do families or families with an above average income. They receive a better education than their peers, and have little responsibility. They are generally brought up in an upper-middle class environment. How can such a movement find opportunity to spread in a country like Turkey, where the majority of the population is Muslim? What do these young people lack that impels them to adopt a movement like Satanism? How can a move-

ment that originated among the children of Western proletarian families become popular among children of wealthy Muslim families? Who spreads Satanism among our young people and how? Most important of all, why do the young commit suicide for the sake of Satan? People are questioning the reasons that lie behind these incidents. This article will look into the answers to these questions as impartially as possible.

How Does Satanism Spread?

Of the factors that help in the spread of Satanism in countries like Turkey, computers and the Internet are at the fore. It is striking that young people who are interested in Satanism are mostly high school students. As most of these young people have learnt a foreign language, they can easily gain access to Satanism via the computer and the Internet. Those who want to learn about Satanism first turn to these resources. It is also known that there are people, with evil intentions, who intentionally encourage young people to become Satanists. The information

given in documents and books on Satanism (verified by what happens in practice) indicates that there are some people who are trying to tempt young people into being Satanists, intentionally and systematically. I do not think that either non-Satanists, or those who claim to be Satanists in Muslim dominated countries, really know what Satanism is, which is quite natural. However, venturing blindly into an unknown subject may lead to unexpected results. The young people who were drawn to suicide, who were raped or murdered, are the bitterest indications of this. Insufficient information and ignorance are among the leading reasons for the spread of Satanism among young people. What one must ask here is why the young people in these countries want to become Satanists.

Why Do Young People Become Satanists?

Of the answers received to this question asked to young people who claim to be Satanists, the following are especially striking: *I became a Satanist because I was angry with God who took away my parents when I was little. I became a Satanist to be a Satanist. I joined the Satanists because I was looking for peace. I sold my soul to Satan because I understood that it was meaningless to live in this world and that I did not belong here. I wanted more freedom.* As can be seen, some young people are angry with God, because of some loss or hardship that they experienced as small children. Some do not even know why they became Satanists. Some look for peace, purpose or freedom in such a cult that they cannot find in their families. Satanism seems attractive to these young people as it encourages them to be rebellious and reactionary against the principles and institutions around them. The answers given above demonstrate that behind the problem of Satanism lies a lack of spiritual knowledge and education. If young people are taught correctly about God, Who created man as an honorable creature and placed him above all living things, they would learn not to be angry with God and would not side with Satan. Similarly, if they are taught that man was not created in vain, that life and creation serve a purpose, that even man himself does not have the right to take his own life, that such an action incurs terrible consequences, and that there is another world in the Hereafter, they would not desire to end their lives and they would not conceive of life in this world as being meaningless.

Another important point to be made is that no precautions are being taken to combat Satanism, despite the fact that young people are being drawn into this spiritual abyss. They are clearly embroiled in a quest for happiness. They are searching for satisfaction everywhere: in the family, at school, in the community, and in society. Here the question regarding what type of young people join Satanist cults springs to mind.

Which Groups Tend More toward Satanism?

Research shows that there are certain groups of young people who are more likely to be drawn into Satanism. Some of these are as follows: children from broken homes or dysfunctional families, or children who are neglected or not given the necessary care by their parents. Children who have trouble establishing relationships with their peers and are therefore cast out by their friends and environment, leaving them lonely and vulnerable are also at risk. Children who are not supported or cared for by society and those who have difficulty in the full realization of their identities or personalities, and who are therefore pushed into depression, are vulnerable. Young people with spiritual or psychological problems, those who have failed to overcome the problems of adolescence and therefore suffer from depression, are often targeted by such groups, while those who are trying to find themselves by joining different groups and by being different from others, and those with a rebellious spirit, who rightly or wrongly react against their family, their environment, and their teachers, are easily persuaded to join such groups. Sometimes those born with some disability or who are challenged in some way can rebel against God. On the other hand, those who are financially satisfied, healthy and sound, but who are spiritually hungry, and therefore seeking fulfillment, can often be misled. Sometimes, young people can go astray merely due to their adventurous spirits, or their curiosity, or simply because they have not been given a sound religious education. Moreover, some young people unintentionally fall into Satanism without being aware of its nature, becoming ensnared by their boyfriends or girlfriends.

Research also reveals that a great majority of young people who tend toward Satanism and commit suicide for its sake are either high school students or of such an age. This leads to the question as to why students at high-school tend more toward Satanism? This can be answered as follows: the ages of the young people who tend toward Satanism range from 14 to 20. In Turkey, this range extends to 25. However, as the ages of 14 to 20 correspond to the high school years, the tendency to move toward Satanism is more likely to be seen in this age group, the years of adolescence. During this period, some physical and psychological changes occur in young people, a phenomenon that can lead to several spiritual and psychological problems. Since this age group is emotionally sensitive, these young people are more susceptible to influence and direction. They react emotionally when they make friends or join groups, and they cannot always make logical decisions on whether the friends or the groups that they are joining are sound or not. At the same time, the ages of 14 to 20 are the years when young people form their identities. Consequently, one of the main reasons why young people at high school tend toward Satanism is the fact that they have not yet fully developed their personality, and some are suffering from some sort of identity crisis. This is also a period when individuality and freedom gain priority, and young people become more reactionary, looking for an alternative lifestyle, something that may be shocking to the older generation. Young people at this stage in their life are easily influenced by events.

Medication, Pregnancy and God's Will

■ Pavel A. Kovganko

Pregnancy is a unique condition for women, and childbirth has always been considered to be one of the most important events in a woman's life. Maternity has always been highly respected and esteemed. People have always regarded the birth of a child as a gift from God.

A wanted child brings happiness to a family; it is a gift from God. And, of course, every woman who wants to give birth wants to bring up a healthy and beautiful child. Unfortunately, the health index of the modern generation of women at child-bearing age is not very high (there are many chronic diseases, spiritual poverty, with a high vulnerability to different infections due to a variety of reasons). Due to this reason, medical interference in what is a natural process has become more frequent recently. Statistics show that more than 92% of women use different drugs at different stages of pregnancy. The question is to what extent this medication is safe for the future baby. This is a fundamentally important matter to investigate because a pregnant woman taking any chemicals is in essence applying a kind of experiment on herself as well as to the baby's health which can have a variety of different consequences.

The problem of medical effects on the development of a fetus has recently become very acute. This is because there are many different medications that are common and easily available nowadays, and they are very often taken without a doctor's prescription. Unfortunately, the consequences of this fact are not pleasant. Prenatal development is one of the most important and difficult stages in a person's life. In just 9 months, an ovicell (an egg cell) and a sperm cell form an extremely complex living organism that consists of millions and billions of cells! Moreover, all these cells are combined into tissues, organs and systems that are always interacting. The fetus has a fascinating rate of growth to become a structure with an ever-increasing complexity. In addition, all these processes do not happen chaotically but in a strict order. This order is supplied by

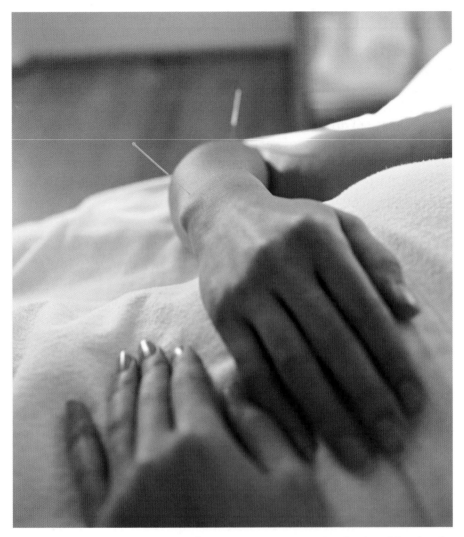

two factors: the first is a sound genetic program. It is obtained by the fetus from its parents and the decoding of the genome vividly denotes the existence of Divine Power. The second factor is the state of a maternal organism which supplies everything necessary for the realization of the genetic program and protects the fetus from the negative influence of the environment. In this way the failure of one of the mentioned factors can lead to different deviations and to the disturbance of the development, including the formation of congenital malformations of the fetus and even prenatal death.

The history of medicine shows that medications can be the most harmful etiological factor in relation to the fetus. Today, there are many examples proving this fact. One of the best-known examples is the thalidomide tragedy that happened in Europe in the 1950-60s. As a result of taking a poorly studied medicine (a light tranquilizer), the children of hundreds (!) of women were born with serious physical defects. Unfortunately, the list of drugs that causes fetal malformation is not short. Nowadays doctors are aware of syndromes caused by hydantoin, warfarin, aminopterin, and many other medications. Each of these has a specific effect on the fetus (mostly leading to serious abnormalities) when taken by a pregnant woman. In the past, people believed that such children were marked by Satan. But nowadays we say that it is the unpredictable effect of medicine on the realization of the Creator's program. Medical interference can lead to a disruption in the rate of development and affect the order of differentiation in the tissues and organs of fetus. Moreover, drugs can interrupt the blood circulation in the placenta, change the metabolic process between the fetus and the mother, causing a retardation of intrauterine growth or premature labor, or they can be the reason for a falloff in the health of the child in the first years of life.

The influence of drugs on the fetus depends on different factors, such as the term of gestation at which the drug is administered, the dosage, and the length of time that the medicine is taken, as well as the ways that the drug is excreted, the health of the mother and her inherited sensitivity to medicine, and, of course, the properties of the medicine itself. There are many drugs whose influence on the fetus have not yet been examined, as such research is very difficult, expensive, or in many cases, simply impossible. If we understand this, we can see that the outlook for scientific interference in God's creation of human beings is not good.

You may wonder why the wide-spread usage of medication by pregnant women throughout the whole world has not lead to a continuous increase in congenital malformations if it is really this dangerous. Thanks to a happy concourse of circumstances, this process has not become too wide-spread, as there are many factors that allow the fetus to "escape" medical danger. For example, there may be an inherited insensitivity on the part of the fetus to the influence of different medications, the placenta has its own inherent protective function, the medication may be taken in a small dosage, the developmental stage of the fetus may be at a "non-critical" period, plus many other factors. Doubtless—although this has not been proven—is the fact that the mother has a sincere faith in God and believes in God's protection of her and her child, which has a positive influence on the development of the fetus. The initial clustering of embryonic cells and the formation of all the fetus' organs and systems occur in the first trimester of pregnancy. It is particularly in this period that the fetus is very sensitive to the influence of different factors, including different drugs.

It is quite common that the results of the use of some teratogens[4] by pregnant women, which can have fatal effects, can simply go unnoticed in some cases, resulting in the death of the fetus during the first two weeks of development. In this case, the woman does not even know that she is pregnant. Such cases are not rare (according to some researchers, up to 70% of all pregnancies finish in the early death of the fetus).

What should a pregnant woman do if she is ill or feeling unwell? How can she effectively help herself and minimize the risk of any medications on her baby at the same time? It is never a good idea to self-medicate if you are pregnant, particularly in the case of little-known or untested medications. In any case, it is better to consult an experienced doctor or pharmacist. If for some reason this is impossible, please read the prospectus which is to be found with the medicine carefully. Which dangers the medicine can cause are probably mentioned on the prospectus, and it may be written that the drug should not be used if pregnant. If a drug has been used while being unaware of pregnancy (for example, during the first 2 weeks) then immediately consult a specialist about any possible negative effects there might be for the fetus as soon as you found out that you are pregnant. Going to see your doctor early will allow you the necessary time to avoid any dangers and allow you to arrive at a decision about this pregnancy. If the medication has been prescribed by a doctor then be sure to ask about possible unwanted side effects for the fetus. Don't hesitate to ask such questions. If it seems to you that your doctor's attitude to this question is not serious enough (unfortunately, this happens quite often) then consult a competent specialist (a geneticist or a clinical pharmacist).

---

4   Agents such as drugs, chemicals and infections that can cause birth defects when a mother is exposed to them during pregnancy.

If you are just planning your pregnancy, then try to predict all the negative factors beforehand. If you have some chronic diseases which may become acute during the pregnancy, or if you have an allergic predisposition or high sensitivity to acute respiratory diseases, then you should consult a doctor. Preventive methods which have been worked out especially for you minimize the risk of the illness and the risk of using drugs that are potentially harmful to the fetus. During early stages of ontogenesis the fetus has almost no adaptation mechanisms or specific reactions in its response to the influence of pathogenic agents. Only with time will the fetus' main organs and systems become mature and the functions of the placenta fully form the morphological and functional backgrounds of the response characteristics peculiar to a new-born baby. We usually say that everything happens according to God's Will but He has created us for a full, vivid, and creative life. And He wants us to understand and be attentive to the miracle that happens during pregnancy.

Peer Instruction: A Better Way to Learn

■ Ertan Salık

Teaching and learning are two common human activities. If we need to name a great difference between humans and animals, this is the one. As Nursi points out,[5] almost from the very moment of birth an animal seems to have been trained and perfected elsewhere, whereas people are born knowing nothing of life and their environment and so must learn everything. Learning more and the correct things improve one's life. So, we are all concerned with how we can learn more efficiently, and, in turn, how we can teach more efficiently.

Education becomes more formal at school. There are a great many different teaching styles inspired by different educational philosophies. Likewise, there are very many learning styles based on different personalities. Every person is created differently and every person may have a slightly different learning style. However, at schools where mass teaching is done, teachers need to decide on a certain method. There are some traditional methods and some novel ones. Here we will focus on peer instruction[6], a non-traditional teaching method developed over the last decade based on physics education research, and later applied in other science teaching as well. We will also try to extract lessons from the peer instruction experience to guide us not only in learning in the classroom but also in everyday informal learning practices.

Eric Mazur is a professor of physics at Harvard University. About a decade ago, Mazur discovered that his students could not correctly answer seemingly simple qualitative questions, despite being able to work through much more difficult quantitative problems. He was shocked as he was considered to be one of the best instructors in the physics department. Mazur began to document the disparity between

5   Nursi, Said. *The Words*, New Jersey: The Light, 2005, pp 331–332
6   http://mazur-www.harvard.edu/research/detailspage.php?ed=1&rowid=8

student performance on the two types of questions, by including on his exams paired qualitative and quantitative questions on a single physics-based concept. He soon confirmed that for his students, success in solving traditional physics problems did not imply that they understood the underlying physics. Many physics instructors across the United States shared Professor Mazur's experience. Mazur started developing what is now known as peer instruction.

As the name suggests, peer instruction promotes learning through interaction with one's peers in the classroom, in addition to listening to the instructor. This is very new, considering that many remember science classes in the form of a plain lecture, where the only player is the instructor, and the students are the audience, except for a few outgoing students who are not always appreciated by their peers. Peer instruction transforms the students into active players during the class. This is actually common sense in all our education experiences. If you just listen to an idea, you will understand very little, and retain very little. If you think about the subject matter, try to apply it in different circumstances, and finally teach it to someone else, then your chance of comprehension and retention greatly improves. This is what the instructor achieves through peer instruction. The students are gently pushed toward thinking, discussing, and finally teaching each other, and so they learn more and better.

Every class in peer instruction includes three or four mini-lectures followed by (or sometimes preceded by) a conceptual question. Students are assigned prior reading so as to come to the class prepared and to have at least some familiarity with the new concepts and terminology. Each mini-lecture's goal is to highlight certain concepts and give the students further insight. Very different from traditional physics lectures, the instructor does not feel obligated to solve many example problems where a lot of math is needed. That is done through homework and during the problem sessions, which are usually administered by teaching assistants. Between mini-lectures, three to five conceptual questions are distributed. Each conceptual question is a qualitative multiple-choice question that gives students and the instructor a means to assess what students have learned. Most questions are asked twice. In the first stage, the instructor shows the question on a projector screen and reads it aloud. Each student is asked to think individually about the answer. No talking is allowed. At the end of this first one or two-minute period, the instructor asks the students to show their responses. This can be done with flashcards, or electronic transmitters (clickers). A flashcard may have the choices (A, B, C, etc.), or the instructor may prefer to use color flashcards. Some schools provide students with clickers (or students buy them), and the instructor has the receiver that is connected to a computer.

After receiving the answers from the students, the instructor assesses the situation. If there are only a few correct answers, then the question was asked prematurely. If there are only a few incorrect answers, then the question was too easy, no more time is devoted to that concept. However, in most cases the instructor selects a question to which 30–70% of the answers will be correct. Then, in the second stage, without giving the correct answer, the instructor asks the students to turn to their peers sitting next to them, and discuss the answer and its reasoning. This is peer instruction. These interactions between students have proven very useful. At the end of the second stage, which typically lasts two to three minutes, the instructor asks the students to show their responses to the same question once again. It has been shown that most of the time the number of correct answers goes up. Clearly, success is conditional on the pre-class reading, a mini-lecture that highlights the concepts, and selection of the carefully designed conceptual questions. Based on the responses, the instructor can decide whether to elaborate on the topic or proceed to something new.

Below is a conceptual question[7] that may be asked while studying the law of gravitation.

---

7   Eric Mazur, *Peer Instruction: A User's Manual*. Prentice-Hall, Upper Saddle River, NJ, 1997

1. The Moon does not fall to Earth because:
a. it is in the Earth's gravitational field.
b. the net force on it is zero.
c. it is beyond the main pull of the Earth's gravity.
d. it is being pulled by the Sun and planets as well as by the Earth.
e. All of the above.
f. None of the above.

At this point we suggest that the reader should think about this question before reading the next paragraph, which includes the correct answer at the end. If possible, ask someone near you and discuss your reasoning. This question is carefully designed with choices representing various misconceptions. For example, any student with some introductory knowledge of physics will accept that if the net force on an object is zero, then the object will not move, so it is tempting for some students to say, "Oh, yes. The Moon does not fall to Earth. This means that the net force on it is zero!" Or, "everybody has a direct experience of the gravitational pull of the Earth. You jump and you fall to Earth. You cannot escape." Again, it is tempting to say that the Moon is beyond the main pull of the Earth's gravity, but that is not true because if there were not enough gravitational force on the Moon, it would escape the Earth's orbit. Option 4, for example, is correct as a statement. By virtue of having a mass, the moon is pulled by the Sun and other planets. One might tend to think that there is a balance between the gravitational forces applied by the Earth and other heavenly objects. But no, that is not the actual reason for the Moon not to fall to Earth. None of the options alone gives the correct answer. Since two of the options (2 and 3) are incorrect, the correct answer to this question is option 6, "None of the above." The correct answer is that the Moon orbits the Earth as well as being pulled by its gravitational force. The reason the Moon keeps changing its direction is the gravitational pull of the Earth. The Moon was given an initial speed so that it does not fall. If the Moon should stop at any instant, it would fall to Earth.

To reiterate our main point, peer instruction causes students to think through and apply a general principle to different cases through conceptual questions and teach each other what they have just learned. That is, our brain becomes much more active, and it is forced to synthesize different pieces of information, rather than keeping busy with factual information only. Research has shown that peer instruction improves the learning gains of the students greatly[8-9-10-11]. Peer instruction has been used in astronomy, chemistry, biology, and mathematics as well. How can we benefit from the peer instruction experience to improve our everyday teaching and learning practices? Before trying to answer this question, let us remember occasions when we learn and teach in our daily lives. We teach and learn when we talk to our friends. When we browse through a newspaper, listen to the radio, or watch a TV program, we are bombarded with information. We read books hoping to learn something from them.

The first message we should receive from the success of peer instruction is that passive listening and watching only injects a lot of information in a short time into our memories. Because such information is not processed with an active mind, or we do not try to apply it in different situations, we should be aware that such information might not be so reliable in general. The irony is that many people in the twenty-first century look to the TV, movies, and radios for information. On the TV screen we see twenty-four pictures every second, that is, about a quarter million pictures daily, if we watch TV for three hours per day. In order for TV and radio to be useful, as peer instruction shows, viewers and listeners need to stop and think about what they have just seen and listened to. If possible, then turn to a friend, discuss what you have just watched and get their opinion. Try to teach what you have just learned and see the reaction of people around you.

When we read, we have more time to think. We should gently push our brains to make connections with what we know, and what we have just read. What is the purpose? What is the message? Why is this significant? Then again, try to teach it to a friend, enter into a short discussion. This can really help minimize misconceptions and refine our understanding. It will help us assimilate the information, and make it our own. As Nursi puts it, "A learned guide should be a sheep not a bird. A sheep gives its lamb milk, while a bird gives its chick regurgitated food[12]." Yes, we should try to digest information, and our chances of digesting it improves with continuous thought, meaningful discussions, and when we try to teach someone else, just like what happens in peer instruction.

8   D. Meltzer, and K. Manivannan, *Am. J. Phys.* 70, June 2002
9   Mark C. James, *Am. J. Phys.* 74, August 2006
10 Catherine H. Crouch and Eric Mazur, Am. J. Phys. 69, September 2001.
11 T. J. Bensky, *Am. J. Phys.* 71, November 2003
12 Nursi, Said, *The Letters*, New Jersey: The Light, 2007, pp 445–458

Honoring Our Parents

■ Fatih Harpçı

O ur parents are the people who provide the most care for us in this world. Unfortunately, most of us often fail to show them the respect they deserve. There are many days set aside in societies to honor and appreciate parents; Father's Day and Mother's Day to name just two. Such days appear to be more an effort to make up for duties neglected. In Monotheistic religions—when they are practiced—respecting, honoring and appreciating parents is not something that should be just one day a year, but rather on each and every day. In Islam, parents' rights are the most venerable rights after those of God. There are many verses in the Qur'an urging Muslims to treat their parents with utmost kindness, to be grateful for the care they have provided, to obey them, and to care for them when they grow old.

> Now (among the good deeds), We have enjoined on human is the best treatment towards his parents. His mother bore him in pain, and in pain did she give him birth. The bearing of him and suckling of him (until weaned) is thirty months. When he has finally reached his full manhood and reached forty years of age, he says: "My Lord! Arouse me that I may be thankful for all Your favors (life, health, sustenance, faith, and submission, and more) that You have bestowed on me and on my parents, and that I may do good, righteous deeds with which You will be pleased, and grant me righteous offspring (so that they treat me righteously, as I treat my parents). I have turned to You, and I am one of those who have submitted to You." Those are they from whom We will accept (their good deeds in a manner to reward them in accordance with) the best of what they ever did, and whose evil deeds We will overlook, (and include them) among the companions of Paradise. This is a true promise which they have been given (here in the world). (al-Ahqaf 46:15–16)

One point that should be emphasized here is that while both parents are given importance, the mother ranks before the father in Islam as far as their children are concerned. God's Messenger said: "Paradise lies under the feet of the mother." However, fathers are never ignored: "The contentment of the father is the door to paradise."

The teachings of Jesus are no different. The Qur'an describes the miracle of baby Jesus speaking out to prove his blessed mother's chastity; when Jesus mentions God's blessings on him, he also emphasizes the importance of being good to one's parents: *...And (God has made me) dutiful towards my mother, and He has not made me unruly, wicked.* (Maryam 19:32). Also, one of the Ten Commandments says: *"Honor your father and your mother"* (Exodus, 20:12). The word "honor" cannot only be defined as feeding parents, clothing them, and helping them get from point A to B, because these are acts of charity usually reserved for homeless or poor people. "Honor" means to prize highly, show respect, glorify, or exalt. From the very moment of conception, and as the child grows and develops, it is a duty and responsibility for the parents. It is not possible to estimate the depth of attachment or compassion parents feel for their children nor to calculate the troubles or hardships they undergo as parents. For this reason, respecting the parent is not only a debt of human gratitude; it is also a religious obligation.

Those who can value their parents in the correct way and who regard them as a means for obtaining the mercy of God are the most prosperous in both worlds. Those who, in contrast, regard their parents' existence as a burden on themselves or who become wearied of them are unfortunate people who will inevitably suffer the severest hardships in life. The more respectful you are to your parents, the greater the respect and awe you will feel before your Creator. Those who do not feel or show respect to their parents have no fear, awe, or respect of God. However, it is a curious thing today that it is not only those who are disrespectful to God who fail to show respect to their parents, but also those who claim that they love God. As Martin Luther expressed, we must respect and love God so that we will neither look down upon our parents or superiors, nor irritate them, but rather we will honor them, serve them, obey them, love them, and value them.

The importance of respecting parents, however, extends beyond social welfare to the very welfare of society itself, as the family is the basic unit of society. Just as a body's health is dependent on the health of the cells, so too is the vigor of a nation, the body politic, directly related to the health of the families that make it up. Families form the foundation of a society. Where there is reciprocal respect of rights and obligations within a family, the society will be healthy and strong. It is vain to look for compassion and respect in society once these have been lost. Fethullah Gülen refers to this neglected value in the following words:

> How we treat our parents can be taken as an indication of how our children will learn to treat us. Obviously, we too hope to become old. If we do not honor our parents, then in keeping with the maxim: "Let the punishment fit the crime," our children will not be dutiful towards us. If we treasure life in the Hereafter, this is an important treasure for us: Let us be dutiful towards our parents and win their pleasure. However, if it is this world that we love, still let us try to please them, so that through them our life will be easy and our sustenance plentiful. If we want the mercy of the Most Merciful One, we should be merciful towards those in our house who He has entrusted to us.

There are different types of parents, but regardless of how they treat their children, they are still parents. Parents make mistakes too, but that does not decrease their value. While we are still under parental guidance we have to follow what they want, even if it goes against our heart. When we are standing on our own two feet, then we have freedom, but we still have the responsibility to respect our parents. We have to examine the situation, rather than concentrating on our own satisfaction. We have to be kind to our parents, because most of the things they do are for us.

Today it is likely that parents are more neglected than in any other period throughout history, even though modern life has provided us with more and more comforts. Said Nursi drew attention to another aspect of the issue in *The Gleams*:

> There have been many experiences that have given me the certain conviction that, in the same way that infants are sent their sustenance in a wonderful fashion by Divine Mercy because of their impotence, flowing forth from the springs of their mothers' breasts, so too the sustenance of the believing elderly, who have acquired innocence, is sent in the form of miraculous abundance. The part of a hadith which says, "Were it not for the elderly with their bent backs, calamities would descend on you in floods," makes clear that a family's source of abundance is the elderly among it, and it is the elderly who preserve the family from the visitation of calamities.

Since the weakness and powerlessness of old age are the means of attracting Divine Mercy to this extent; since the wise Qur'an through the verses, *Should one of them, or both, attain old age in your lifetime, do not say 'Ugh!' to them (as an indication of complaint or impatience), nor push them away; and always address them in gracious words. Lower to them the wing of humility out of mercy, and say: "My Lord, have mercy on them even as they cared for me in childhood."* (al-Isra 17:23–24) calls children, in the most wonderfully eloquent fashion, in five ways to be kind and respectful towards their elderly parents; since the religion of Islam orders respect and compassion towards the elderly; since human nature also requires respect and compassion towards the elderly, we elderly people certainly enjoy, in place of the temporary physical pleasures roused by appetites of youth, substantial, continual mercy and respect from Divine grace and human innate feelings of tenderness, and the contentment of spirit that arises from such respect and compassion. This being the case, we should not wish to exchange this old age of ours for a hundred youths. I can tell you certainly that if they were to give me ten years of the Old Said's youth, I would not give in exchange one year of the New Said's old age. I am content with my old age, and you too should be content with yours (The Twenty-Sixth Gleam, Ninth Hope).

Elderly believers are more deeply aware that the true abode is the Eternal One, and turn to God with sincere devotion. Therefore, they present an example to the younger generations with their piety, wisdom, and tolerance. In short, even though we respect our parents for the sake of God, observing their rights and caring for them not only leads to eternal happiness in the Hereafter, but it also provides us with such an inner peace no worldly pursuit can bring. To put it in religious terminology, abiding by the Divine commands results in *saadat al-darayn*—happiness in both abodes.

References

Adil, Furkan. *Kudsi İki Varlık: Anne-Baba*, istanbul: Rehber Yayınları, 2008.

Gönüllü, Ömer Said. "Ebeveyn Hukuku ve İnsan Olma," *Sızıntı*, 298.

Gülen, Fethullah, *Fasıldan Fasıla 3*, İstanbul: Nil Yayınları, 1997.

Luther, Martin. *Martin Luther's Large and Small Catechism*. Translated by F. Benteand W.H.T. Dan. Sioux Falls, SD: Nuvision Publications, 2007.

Nursi Said. *The Gleams*, "Solace for the Elderly," New Jersey: Tughra Books, 2008.

Taiwo, Niyi. *Respect: Gaining It and Sustaining It*. Philadelphia, PA: Xlibris Corporation, 2007.

Ünal, Ali. *The Qur'an with Annotated Interpretation in Modern English*, New Jersey: The Light, 2006.

The Education of Gifted Children

■ Hayati Tarhan

Humans are created with different levels of ability. A person who is talented in one specific field may not necessarily be as capable in other areas, and individuals who have natural ability in the same field do not necessarily have the same level of ability because some children are born with an outstanding natural talent. Therefore, the division of labor in communities is shaped accordingly and opportunities are sought for the development of skills. Unfortunately, while some governments and nations recognize the varying abilities of humans and provide education and facilities accordingly, others show no concern for the educational requirements of gifted children. Discovering the giftedness of children in the early stages of education is very important. If they pass unnoticed, this can be a great loss, and may even result in harmful consequences for individuals and their communities. People with extraordinary talent can play a huge role in the development of communities, the course of history, and in the progress of technology, science, and the arts.

Who Are Gifted Students?

Gifted students display distinctive qualities in many ways. They usually think differently than their friends; they can come up with extraordinary ideas and self-developed thoughts; details are important for them; they have the ability to learn quickly and progress in academic and intellectual fields; they display high performance in one or more types of art. However, these talented people only make up 2% of the society. These individuals do not like to overexert themselves to increase their grades in education, nor do they study in a systematic manner or do homework. They tend to choose practical solutions, produce new ideas, and try to develop these ideas. They analyze and question whatever they learn, but nevertheless they can still be disorganized. They are often the students who cause problems at school. Awkward and disruptive in the classroom, they can be argumentative or uninvolved in activities. Research into the lives of many people who throughout history have caused great change has discovered that the outstanding talent of these famous people usually passed unnoticed by their teachers, and they were actually problematic children in their early years as students. Edison, for example, was taught at home by his mother, an experienced teacher, because he could not conform to or thrive in school life.

To help teachers recognize gifted students, various tests have been introduced into the education systems of schools in the West. One of these exams is the IQ test. Some consider IQ tests as the most efficient way of discovering the abilities of students, while some other educationalists say that the only "skill" an IQ test indicates is the ability to take IQ tests; in fact the more you take, the higher you score. In general, gifted students are recognized by the following qualities:

-They are quick to learn; they understand and learn the topics in which they have greater ability more easily than other pupils, and they comment on or question the information provided.

-They try to improvise on whatever they learn; they ask questions that will assist them in progressing in the topics they learn and constantly try to develop on these subjects.

-They enjoy speaking with older people and usually choose the company of friends older than themselves. They obtain pleasure from discussing with older people, usually teachers.

-They have the ability to judge and transform information.

-They have extraordinary desire for intellectual activity.

-As well as being energetic or overactive, they can also be introverted individuals who prefer their own company.

-They absorb even the tiniest detail in subjects in which they have an interest.

-They study only to satisfy their overwhelming desire to learn, and not to please their families or teachers.

-They are curious, continually asking why and how and other similar questions.

-They have very good memories.

-They easily figure out complex objects and events.

Gifted individuals may have many more qualities than those listed above. Another aspect to consider is that if a child has one or a few of these qualities we should not come to the conclusion right away that he is a gifted child. A child could be talented in one certain topic. An individual who shows outstanding performance in mathematics could be completely unsuccessful in social studies and even worse in art, and a student who is successful in art may be very poor at physics. The understanding that an intelligent student must be successful in every field of education is misleading because this is not the case with all individuals. Further, methods of discovering a student's ability in one field may not be suitable for other subjects.

Types of Education for Gifted Students

In different countries of the world there are various kinds of education for gifted students. These can be categorized as separate education, combined education, and individual education.

1. Separate education: Separate education is grouping students to be educated according to the subjects in which they show higher performance. This kind of education is usually regarded as unsuitable in present-day understandings of schooling on the grounds that if not well balanced, separate education may encourage selfishness, a sense of arrogance and unsound personality.

2. Combined education: This is a form of education where talented individuals continue studies in their usual environment among their friends in the five different formats noted below:

a) Education in special classes: Students known to have a higher rate of ability are taught in special classes in their own schools.

b) Early education: This is enrolling gifted children in schools earlier than the normal school age, usually a year earlier but in some cases maybe even two years, depending on a child's general intellectual performance. This format is not advised because early education is said to have negative effects on the physical, emotional and psychological development of children.

c) Accelerated education: This is where children known to have outstanding intelligence are advanced to a higher class. This can be implemented two times at the most.

d) Groups of equal ability: This is a form of education where students with the same abilities in certain subjects are taught in specific, segregated classes and then encouraged to develop their skills in their topic of interest.

e) Enriched schedule: This is where a skilled individual is provided with special activities in his or her own classroom alongside the normal curriculum.

3. *Individual education*: A student with outstanding abilities is provided with a specific education in their own field of interest.

Recommended Types of Education

If we look at the various kinds of education, the most appropriate forms of learning seem to be groups of equal ability and the enriched schedule because separating children from their usual environment and friends can induce various problems. Education of groups with equal ability is a method where students of equal ability are taught in one class. The ideal number of students per class is three, and a teacher is usually assigned to the class as a counselor.

After lessons the students research the topics relevant to their interests or abilities. This research begins with easier tasks, and while they are investigating the topic, the students are actually learning and practicing different methods of learning. They learn in sequence how to research a topic and what to do when they are faced with a problem. The students learn study and learning methods without realizing that they are actually learning. This is a very effective method, and in this kind of education, students gain the chance to learn and research, develop and innovate while remaining among their friends in their normal environment. Therefore, they are not subjected to the negative aspects of segregation, and gifted students in higher classes become an example for younger, outstandingly gifted students in lower classes.

Education with an Enriched Schedule

In the enriched schedule education program, the student continues his or her usual education in his or her own classroom guided by the teacher to perform research in the field in which he or she has greater ability. He or she then explains the research discoveries to classmates. Thus, while students are developing skills in explaining discoveries, they are also teaching their friends and representing model students in the classroom. Teachers play a big role in this type of education. It is their duty to recognize the students' fields of interest or abilities and arrange a program suitable to the students' characters.

What the Education of a Gifted Student Entails

Gifted students should not be told of their superior capabilities because the word "superior" or "outstanding" could lead to arrogance in the student, which will cause problems with classmates. Students who

think they are superior will begin to think that studying is unnecessary, which could lead to them abandoning their education completely. Nevertheless, their education can be customized according to their greater abilities. Gifted students are individuals who need special education and trained, professional teachers, just like a student with hearing problems, a blind student or a student with a learning impairment.

Conclusion

The main differences between a student of normal learning capacity and one of outstanding abilities are that a gifted student can achieve what others think impossible. A ship being commanded from land, the discovery of electricity, the invention of motor vehicles, priceless classic paintings, music, literature and works of art are all the products of extraordinarily skilled people. Outstanding talent is a gift from God, a great blessing. One who has a gift and the people responsible for discovering it and ensuring it develops, namely the mother, father, and teacher, must recognize it in the early stages and educate these children in a beneficial manner so that they will be able to do work which is of interest to them, work that ordinary people would not be able to do. In this way, they will be able to benefit others as well as themselves. They must also develop in their character and spirituality. If a talented person does not have a good character, he or she could become more dangerous than a person of normal intelligence. Great responsibility lies with teachers and the education authorities.

Abortion: Mercy or Murder?

■ Dr. S. Aksoy

A bortion is the intentional destruction of the fetus in the womb, or any untimely delivery brought about with intent to cause the death of the fetus (Price, 1988). As is evident in the definition, it is the *intention* to terminate the life of a living being which has made abortion such a controversial issue. Hippocrates (c. 3rd century BC) wrote in his famous oath: "I will not give to a woman a pessary to cause abortion" (Reiser et. al. 1977, p.5). The history of abortion goes that far back, perhaps further. How can abortion which contradicts such basic imperatives of medical practice, like "Do not harm" or "Respect human life", be so deep rooted in the history of that practice? What made (and still makes) health professionals carry out abortions on such a wide scale?

Two principal kinds of indications have been defined for "termination of pregnancy". The first, called "medical indications", are: 1) That continuance of the pregnancy would put the life of the pregnant woman at risk, or put her physical or mental health or that of any existing children, at greater risk than if the pregnancy were terminated; 2) There is a substantial risk that if the child were born it would suffer from such physical or mental abnormalities as to be seriously disabled.

The second kind of indications, the so-called "social indications", are more complex and vary between cultures and epochs. Examples are: pregnancies resulting from extra-marital relations, from rape or incest, unwanted or unplanned pregnancies, pregnancies at too young or too old an age, expecting a baby of the "wrong" sex—the information being provided by recent medical technology. We may note that it is primarily "social reasons" of this sort that lead parents to seek abortion. The actual termination of pregnancies has been carried out either by health professionals or by some unqualified person, sometimes even by the pregnant woman herself.

Abortion has always been discussed by doctors, philosophers, lawyers and theologians from different perspectives. Here I shall go over some of these arguments, and try to come to a conclusion about the ethics of abortion. Actually, as Dunstan observes (1978, p. 78), we shall be considering the ethics of a practice already very widespread, and likely to become more so, in all regions of the world, developed and developing. At least fifty million abortions are carried out annually world-wide, and, for example in France and Japan, half of all pregnancies end in abortion (E.B., 1982, vol.2,

p.1069). One and half million abortions are performed in USA each year, one-third of them on teenagers between 12 and 17 years old (Poots & Diggory, 1983, p.287). Therefore, it is rather difficult to discuss the moral acceptability of something which has already been so widely accepted. A 1991 Harris poll showed 81% of adults in England in favor of a woman's right to choose to have an abortion in the first three months of pregnancy (Cole, 1992, p.2) Mason (p.113) states that: "The significant feature is not so much the total number of abortions but, rather, the steady escalation in numbers over the years. The figures indicate that there must be an increasing public acceptance of abortion as a natural way of life". Dunstan (1974, p.87) commenting on this fact writes: "Abortion is now being more widely legalized and practiced because that is what people want—an indication for medical intervention for the destruction of life unknown in our ethics before".

Writers on the abortion issue have concentrated most on two matters: first, the "rights" of the fetus and the mother, in particularly the property right of the woman on her body; second, the question of the "personhood" of the prenate (i.e. the unborn child). Judith Jarvis Thomson is one of the pioneers among writers who approach the issue from the perspective of the "rights" of the fetus and the mother. She has no difficulty recognizing the "personhood" of the fetus. She says every person has a right to life, so the fetus has a right to life. However, she believes that the mother has a right to decide what shall happen in and to her body (Dunstan, 1974, p.203). The "personhood" or legal, moral status of the prenate is a very involved legal, philosophical question which I have addressed elsewhere (see Aksoy, 1996). People who have defined views on the issue generally take one of three positions: 1) abortion is always wrong and must never be performed at any time for any reason; 2) abortion may be carried out at any time for any reason; and 3) abortion should only be allowed up to a certain stage of pregnancy, after which it should not be allowed except under certain special conditions. The people in the first group are not very many. They follow the Roman Catholic teaching which maintains:

"We cannot be absolutely certain when animation takes place, or when the conceptus or the fetus is a human person; but it may well be precisely at the moment of conception. This being so, it would be seriously wrong to destroy the fertilized ovum even then, because one might be killing a human person" (Mahoney, 1984, p.69). According to this strict line, abortion is impermissible even when the mother's life is in danger or the pregnancy is the result of an indecent event, like rape or incest.

The second position is held by those who advance the "personhood" argument. Harris (1990) is one of those writers who suggest that: "A person is a creature capable of valuing its own existence. And non-persons or potential persons cannot be wronged in this way because death does not deprive them of anything they can value. If they cannot wish to live, they cannot have that wish frustrated by being killed." The third position which may be defined as "moderate" maintains that abortion should not be allowed after a certain stage of pregnancy and only if particular circumstances justify it. For instance, it is a very common view that abortion should be permitted in order to save the mother's life. Some people believe that abortion is also morally permissible when pregnancy is the result of rape or incest, and when a severe fetal abnormality has been diagnosed. There are also writers who suggest that termination of pregnancy should be permissible if the potential mother is too young.

One exceptional circumstance which justifies abortion, on this view, is the diagnosis of severe abnormalities in the fetus. The argument is that it is wrong to bring avoidable suffering into the world and we are morally obliged to terminate the life of severely handicapped fetuses. One writer has explained that it is a misconception to regard this justification as "on behalf of" the fetus (Mason, p.106). In reality the suffering being avoided is being avoided on behalf of the mother and other potential caregivers. We need to be clear about whether the termination due to disability is being considered in the supposed interest of the unborn child—that it is "better" for that child not to live at all then to live with a foreseeable handicap—or in the "interest" of those who would have the care and burden of that child's life, including its suffering and pain (Dunstan, 1974, p.84). Williams (1987, p.297) is explicit that abortion on such grounds relates to the welfare of the parents, whose life may be blighted by having to rear a grossly defective child, with perhaps in the background such secondary considerations as costs to the public purse.

For all the debate, the suggestions and counter-suggestions and alternatives, it seems likely that abortion will remain the dilemma it has been for centuries. However, we must bear in mind the fundamental fact that abortion is termination of the life of a living creature. We must approach ending the life of a prenate as cautiously and sensitively as we would ending the life of any other living creature, and we should not end the life of any living being unnecessarily and without very good reason. On the question of the "personhood" of the prenate, we can be sure only that we will never be sure about it, unless we discover some sort of indicator to decide the matter. As the moral status of the prenate is not something material, we need to refer to the authority of metaphysical and transcendental knowledge, and the religions are among these sources. As I have tried to show elsewhere (Aksoy, 1966), not only all religions but also many philosophers from Aristotle onwards have declared that a human being consists of a body and soul. In the religious perspective, the earthly existence of a person ends when the soul departs the body. At the other end of this "silent journey" (Aksoy, 1995), the human person begins when the soul joins the body. We do not know very much about the when and how of the soul's departure, but there are clear statements in the Qur'an about the time and the process of ensoulment. There is also some information related to this in the Talmud, and some detailed explanation in Aquinas's works.

All the scientific (anatomical and physiological) and metaphysical (religious and spiritual) arguments tell us that, if there is a time between conception and birth at which the prenate "enters humanity", "becomes a person", "becomes morally important" or however we call it, it is most likely to be at some time in the eighth week (Aksoy, n.d.). In sum, even at the very beginning of its existence, we owe respect to the unborn, but after eight weeks time to terminate its life should be defined as morally unacceptable.

It may be asked, if the prenate "becomes a real person" after eight weeks, then how do we regard embryos? Donceel (1984, p.15) suggests that, "Although a pre-human embryo cannot demand from us the absolute respect which we owe to the human person, it deserves a very great consideration, because it is a living being, endowed with a human finality. Therefore it seems to me that only very serious reasons should allow us to terminate its existence." Apparently, it is one thing to say that an entity lacks the dignity of being a person in the strict sense of "person",

...

and another thing to say that it does not have any value. The embryo may, in this respect, be regarded as similar to a human corpse. At the moment in question neither of them are existing human persons. The embryo will be one, as the dead body once was. And we owe respect to both. If we mutilate and disgrace a human corpse it is something immoral and shameful, even though not illegal. Similarly, if we destroy or terminate the life of an embryo, it is not an attack on an individual human being but still inhumane and undignified. However, sometimes it might be necessary to undertake an undignified and inhumane action to undo the signs of another "more" undignified and inhumane action, like rape.

The way Dunstan has expressed the dilemma of abortion (1974, p.85–86) gives a most helpful direction to our moral thinking on it; "We should pass from the question, 'what harm are we doing to the fetus by destroying it', to the question, 'what harm are we doing to ourselves, to humanity, when we do so'?"

References:

Aksoy, S. (1995). "The Silent Journey", *The Fountain*, 2 (12), pp. 42–44. (1996). "What makes a person?", *The Fountain*, 14, (n.d.) "When does a human individual begin to be? A philosophical, embryological and theological perspective". (Unpublished paper)

Cole, L. (1992). *My Baby, My Body, My Choice*, Lloyd Cole Books, Maidenhead.

Donceel, J.F. (1984). "A liberal Catholic's view" in Joel Feinberg (ed.) *The Problem of Abortion*, Wodsworth, Belmont CA.

Dunstan, G.R. (1974). *The Artifice of Ethics*, SCM Press Ltd, London.

Encyclopedia Britannica. (1982). 15th ed., Chicago, vol.2, p.1069.

Harris, 1. (1990). "Wrongful birth" in David R. Bromham, Maureen E. Dalton & Jennifer C. Jackson (eds) *Philosophical Ethics in Reproductive Medicine*, Manchester University Press.

Mahoney, J. (1984). *Bio-ethics and Belief*. Sheed & Ward Ltd. London.

Mason, J.K. (1990). *Medicolegal Aspects of Reproduction and Parenthood*, Dartmounth, Hants.

Potts, M. & Diggory, P. (1983). *Textbook of Contraceptive Practice*, Cambridge University Press, New York. Price, D.P. (1988). "Selective reduction and feticide: the parameters of abortion", *Criminal Law Review*, pp. 199–210.

Reiser, S.J., Dyke A.J. & Curran, W.J. (1977). (eds). *Ethics in Medicine: Historical Perspective and Current Concerns*, MIT Press, Cambridge Mass.

Williams, G. (1987). *Textbook of Criminal Law*, Stevens, London.

Index